The UMAP Expository Monograph Series

Spatial Models of Election Competition
Steven J. Brams, *New York University*

Elements of the Theory of Generalized Inverses for Matrices
Randall E. Cline, *University of Tennessee*

Introduction to Population Modeling
James C. Frauenthal, *SUNY at Stony Brook*

Conditional Independence in Applied Probability
Paul E. Pfeiffer, *Rice University*

Topics in the Theory of Voting
Philip D. Straffin, Jr., *Beloit College*

Introduction to Population Modeling

Second printing, 1980

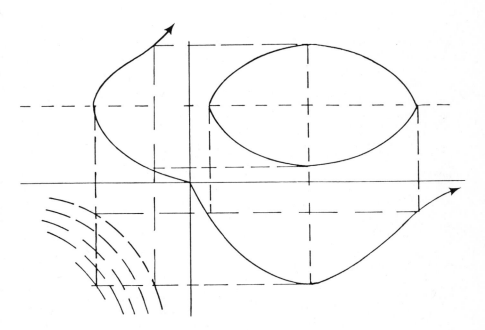

James C. Frauenthal

The Project acknowledges Robert M. Thrall,
Chairman of the UMAP Monograph Editorial
Board, for his help in the development and
review of this monograph.

BIRKHÄUSER

BOSTON • BASEL • STUTTGART

Author

James C. Frauenthal
Applied Mathematics and Statistics
State University of New York
Stony Brook, New York   11794

Library of Congress Cataloging in Publication Data

Frauenthal, J   C
    Introduction to population modeling.

    (UMAP monograph)
    "Lecture notes from a course taught in the
Department of Applied Mathematics and Statistics at
the State University of New York at Stony Brook in
the spring of 1977."
    Bibliography: p.
    Includes index.
    1. Population--Mathematical models.   I.   Title.
II. Series.
HB849.51.F7   304.6'0724   80-23423

CIP-Kurztitelaufnahme der Deutschen Bibliothek

Frauenthal, James C.:
Introduction to population modeling / James
C. Frauenthal. - 2. printing. - Boston, Basel,
Stuttgart : Birkhäuser, 1980.
    (umap)
    ISBN 3-7643-3015-5

  Education Development Center, Inc. 1980
ISBN 3-7643-3015-5
Printed in USA

Dedication:

To my friend and mentor
Lloyd MacG. Trefethen

Table of Contents

Preface

The text of this monograph represents the author's
lecture notes from a course taught in the Department of
Applied Mathematics and Statistics at the State University
of New York at Stony Brook in the Spring of 1977. On
account of its origin as lecture notes, some sections of
the text are telegraphic in style while other portions are
overly detailed. This stylistic foible has not been
modified as it does not appear to detract seriously from
the readability and it does help to indicate which topics
were stressed.

The audience for the course at Stony Brook was composed mostly of fourth year undergraduate and first year
graduate students majoring in the mathematical sciences.
All of these students had studied at least four semesters
of calculus and one of probability; few had any prior experience with either differential equations or ecology. It
seems prudent to point out that the author's background is
in engineering and applied mathematics and not in the biological sciences. It is hoped that this is not painfully
obvious.

The focus of the monograph is on the formulation
and solution of mathematical models; it makes no pretense
of being a text in ecology. The idea of a population is
employed mainly as a pedagogic tool, providing unity and
intuitive appeal to the varied mathematical ideas
introduced. If the biological setting is stripped away,
what remains can be interpreted as topics on the
qualitative behavior of differential and difference
equations.

The topics in the monograph fall quite naturally into
two sections. The first group of models investigate the
dynamics of a single species, with particular interest in
the consequences of treating time and population size in
discrete and continuous terms. The difficulties encountered
as one tries to incorporate increasing reality in the form
of time delays and environmental fluctuations are stressed.
The second group of models study the interaction of two or
more species. After an initial survey of the implications
of competition versus collaboration, a more careful study
is undertaken of the admissible solutions of differential
equations. The final section on complexity and stability
attempts to summarize one of the basic questions in ecology
using many of the ideas which have been developed.

At the end of each topic a number of problems are
listed which provide practice with mathematical concepts
and techniques. It is suggested that during a one semester
course all problems be solved by students. Without this
level of activity the mathematical details can not be
adequately appreciated. Also at the end of each topic is
an annotated list of references. Students should be
encouraged to read at least some of this source material in
its original form. This activity will not only increase the
depth of understanding of the biological points, it will
also help students to develop confidence in their ability to
interpret the writings of professionals from fields outside

of mathematics.

Most of the ideas and models contained in this monograph are not original, and to their creators I owe a debt of gratitude. I would particularly like to express my thanks to two individuals. My attention was first drawn to the mathematical modeling process by George F. Carrier while I was a graduate student at Harvard. At this same time I met Robert M. May whose ideas will be found to pervade this monograph. I would also like to express my sincere appreciation to the Alfred P. Sloan Foundation whose support greatly facilitated the preparation of this monograph.

Stony Brook, N.Y.   James C. Frauenthal
June 1978

Introduction

The central purpose of this monograph is to
investigate how to describe the evolution in time of a
population of reproducing individuals. The individuals
range in complexity from single cell organisms through
plants and lower animals to humans. Ordinarily, as the
complexity of the organism increases, so does the
sophistication of the mathematical model. Further, since
no species lives in total isolation, it will be necessary
to consider the interaction of several populations.

It is important from the outset to recognize that the
models which will be considered are little more than
caricatures of reality. Real ecosystems can be and in fact
are studied by field ecologists. However, valuable insight
can often be gained by looking at the consequences of the
simplifying assumptions which are contained in mathematical
models. It is essential in the process of interpreting
models never to lose sight of the fact that one is not
dealing with reality.

The first six sections of the monograph investigate
the dynamics of a single population, without explicit
regard for other, interacting populations. The first section
is entitled 'Simple Single Species Population Models'.
After a number of basic assumptions are stated and suitable
variables defined, the kinematic relationship between the

variables is deduced. Two possible mathematical forms
for the dynamics are then introduced, and the consequences
determined by mathematical analysis. In anticipation of
more complicated models, the method of linearized stability
analysis is developed.

The second section is called 'Stochastic Birth and
Death Processes'. In this section models are investigated
which treat population size discretely, but only at the
expense of considerable mathematical complication. The
mathematical tools employed in this section include
probability generating functions and expectation operators.
It is discovered that in general the expected value of the
population size in the stochastic model is in fact the same
as the more easily deduced result for the deterministic
model. For this reason, stochastic models are not pursued
further.

The third section is entitled 'A Two Age Group Model',
and contains the development of a model for the growth of
a population of reproducing individuals in which there is
an initial, infertile period prior to reproductive maturity.
Although the model is very simple, it captures certain
human reproductive properties rather well. The model, which
is formulated in terms of difference equations, submits nicely
to graphical analysis.

In the fourth section, 'Time Delayed Logistic Equations',
the idea of time-lags introduced in the previous section is
extended. Instead of considering only the discrete lag
associated with reaching reproductive maturity, a smeared-out
lag is introduced, corresponding with a smooth phenomenon
such as the gradual regeneration of foliage after a year of
excessive foraging by an oversized population of herbivores.
In the process of analyzing the mathematical model, the
Laplace transformation and the significance of the location
of roots in the complex plane are developed.

The fifth section is entitled 'Population Growth in
a Time Varying Environment'. In this section a selection
of models are studied in which time is treated both
discretely and continuously. The effect of fluctuations
in the ability of the environment to support the
population are modeled, and some rather surprising
consequences deduced.

The final section on single species models, 'Stable
Points, Stable Cycles and Chaos' investigates the dynamics
of populations with non-overlapping generations. A
procedure involving directed graphs is employed to
demonstrate a number of unexpected and unusual properties
of non-linear difference equations.

The latter five sections of the monograph investigate
a sequence of increasingly complicated population interactions. In the seventh section, 'Introduction To Two Species
Models: Predator-Prey', one of the most famous mathematical
models of population ecology is developed. Both approximate
and exact solutions are found to the governing pair of non-
linear differential equations, and the inherent inadequacy
of the model is discussed.

In the eighth section, 'Competition and Mutualism',
the model of the previous section is extended. Interestingly,
although the model was unsatisfactory as a description for
predator-prey interaction, it proves to be quite useful for
competitive and mutualistic behavior. In the process of
analyzing the models in this section, Gause's Principle of
Competitive Exclusion is deduced.

The models of the previous two sections are generalized
in the next section which is entitled 'Quadratic Two Species
Population Models'. In the process of studying the general
model, Green's Theorem is employed, and Hilbert's sixteenth
problem is discussed. Here, as in the sixth section of the

monograph, the forefronts of mathematical research are approached.

The tenth section, 'Three Species Competition' extends the model in the eighth section to the case of three competiting species. A whole new class of possible behavior results since three species are able to exhibit non-transitive interactions which are impossible with just two species present.

The final section, 'Complexity vs. Stability' investigates one of the most interesting questions of population ecology. By means of a sequence of models of complex ecosystems, one is led to conclude that arbitrary complexity does not in general lead to increased stability. Although the mathematics is fairly straightforward, the implications have a profound impact on classical ecology theory.

Perhaps an interesting way to motivate the study of ecology and the mathematics of population growth is to look at the record of Canadian Lynx pelt purchases by the Hudson Bay Company over a period of more than a century. The data, which is sketched in the figure on the next page, is drawn from rather complete company records kept during the period in question. Note that the Hudson Bay Company purchased its pelts from trappers who worked throughout the vast region of Canada from Quebec to British Columbia. Perhaps the most immediately obvious feature of the data in the figure is the large amplitude, ten year cycles. The problem is to try to deduce what natural phenomenon might have produced these oscillations. While this problem will not be dealt with directly, it is typical of the problems which form the focus of this monograph.

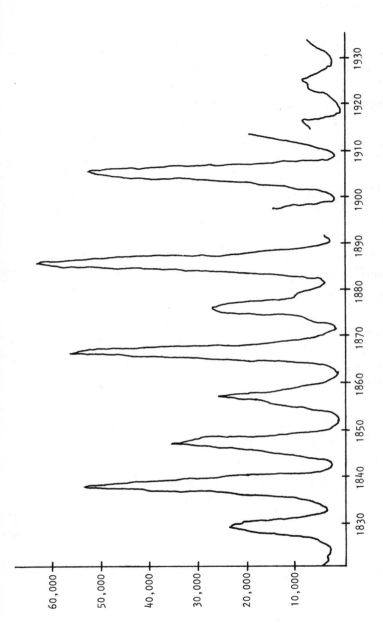

Total number of Lynx pelts purchased by the Hudson Bay Company from the regions of northwestern Canada. Regions omitted from graph correspond with times for which the data is incomplete. A small amount of incomplete data from northeastern Canada has also been omitted. (Original data available in Elton, C. and Nicholson, M., "The ten year cycle in numbers of Lynx in Canada", J. of Animal Ecology, 11 (1942).)

References:

Although it is not customary to provide references to an Introduction, the ones listed below provide further stimulation and encouragement.

Coleman, C.S., "Biological Cycles and the Five-Fold Way", MAA Workshop on Modules in Applied Mathematics, Cornell University, 1976.

The first three sections of this teaching module are the source of the brief account of the Canadian Lynx cycles. The latter portion of the module should not be attempted until after the material in the monograph is successfully mastered. (To acquire this module, see the note in the references to the section entitled Quadratic Population Models.)

May, R.M., Stability and Complexity in Model Ecosystems, Princeton University Press, Princeton, N.J., 1973.

Chapter 2 of this book provides a lucid discussion of mathematical models and stability. The ideas expounded are central to the material in this monograph.

Maynard Smith, J., Models in Ecology, Cambridge University Press, Cambridge, 1974.

Chapter 1 of this book investigates in general terms a number of the questions which occupy the pages of this monograph.

1 Simple Single Species Population Models

We will start by looking at some simple models for the growth of an animal population. The models which we consider are not intended to be very realistic. Instead, by their simplicity, they illustrate a number of the difficulties which arise typically in building mathematical models.

Consider a population of a single species of animals. Let us make a few assumptions:

1. All animals in the population have identical ecological properties (i.e. all are equally likely to give birth, to die, ...). Note that this does away with two very basic properties: age and sex.

2. All animals respond instantaneously to alterations in their environment (i.e. no time lags are required to conform to changes in the environment).

3. No migration is allowed and no animals get lost. Thus the only way to enter the population is to be born (or else to be present

when the model starts) and the only way to
leave is to die.

Let the independent variable be time t, and let

$N(t)$ = the number of animals present at time t.

b = the average number of offspring born per
animal in the population per unit of time.

d = the fraction of animals in the population
which die per unit of time.

Given that at time t there are $N(t)$ animals present,
how many will there be a very short time Δt later? This
number $N(t + \Delta t)$ clearly equals the number present at time
t plus the number born during the time interval less the
number which die. Thus

$$N(t + \Delta t) = N(t) + bN(t)\Delta t - dN(t)\Delta t.$$

N.B.   In general $N(t + \Delta t)$ will not be an integer, even if
$N(t)$ was an integer. Since animals come in integer
units we get around this by demanding that the population is large and interpreting the results to the
nearest integer. This will not introduce serious
percentage errors.

Rearrange the equation to get

$$\frac{N(t + \Delta t) - N(t)}{\Delta t} = (b - d)N(t).$$

N.B.   Since only the difference b - d appears, it is customary to define the Intrinsic Rate of Population
Growth as r = b - d.

Next, let Δt approach 0 to get

$$\frac{dN(t)}{dt} = rN(t).$$

This is an ordinary differential equation which tells the
size of the population at time t, assuming the size is
known at some prior time. Assume that at t = 0 the size
is $N(0) = N_0$ (known).

We must look more closely at the Intrinsic Rate of Population Growth, r. Recognize that in general, r = r(N,t).

Case 1: As a first assumption, let $r = r_0$ (a constant).

Solve: $\dfrac{dN}{dt} = r_0 N$: $N(0) = N_0$.

Method: Separate variables and integrate, to obtain

$$\int_{N_0}^{N(t)} d\tilde{N}/\tilde{N} = r_0 \int_0^t d\tilde{t}$$

$$N(t) = N_0 \exp\{r_0 t\}.$$

As a function of time, this looks like:

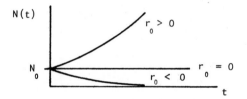

Case 2: For most animal populations, as the population size increases the birth rate decreases and the death rate increases, both due largely to crowding and privation. We will model this by a linearly declining Intrinsic Rate of Population Growth with increasing population size

$r = r(N) = r_0(1 - N/K)$: r_0, K positive constants.

Thus as a function of N, r(N) looks like:

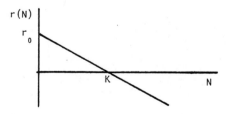

N.B.   Case 1 would be just a horizontal line at level r_0.

Substituting the assumed form of r(N) into the D.E. leads us to the following situation:

Solve: $\dfrac{dN}{dt} = r_0 N(1 - \dfrac{N}{K})$: $N(0) = N_0$.

Method: Although this is a Non-linear D.E. (ordinarily hard to solve) we can again separate variables and integrate

$$\int_{N_0}^{N(t)} d\hat{N}/\{\hat{N}(1-\hat{N}/K)\} \;=\; r_0 \int_0^t d\hat{t}.$$

Expand the denominator of LHS by partial fractions (or use a table of integrals). A straight-forward calculation produces

$$N(t) \;=\; \frac{N_0 \exp\{r_0 t\}}{1 + \dfrac{N_0}{K}\{\exp(r_0 t) - 1\}}.$$

This D.E. is so well known it has a name, the Logistic Equation, and its solution is called the Sigmoid curve. Before plotting the results let us see what we can learn by looking at limiting behavior:

1.   When $K \to \infty$, the denominator goes to unity, and the solution becomes the same as the result for Case 1.

2.   When $t \to \infty$, since $r_0 > 0$, exponentials dominate, and $N \sim K$, regardless of the value of N_0.

In other words, for finite K, the solution always ends up at K. Ecologists call K the Carrying Capacity of the environment.

For two different initial population sizes, one with $N_0 > K$, the other with $N_0 < K$ the solution looks like:

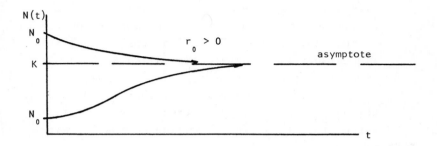

We found the solution by solving the D.E. However, this is not always possible. We therefore would like to find a method for interpreting our model even if it is not possible to solve the D.E. We will now develop a method for doing this. It will provide us with observations 1 and 2 above, without finding a complete solution.

This procedure for learning about the solution without solving the equation is called Stability Analysis (or sometimes Perturbation Analysis). It can frequently be employed when confronted by a Non-linear D.E.

Stability Analysis: The procedure consists of first finding all the equilibrium points. Once these are known, we then determine the stability of each one separately. Note that the method breaks down if there are no equilibrium points.

Before studying how to ask these questions mathematically, we review the concepts of equilibrium and stability.

> Equilibrium: A functional, though neither general nor precise definition is that a system (population) is in equilibrium for all values of the dependent variable (N) which are such as to render the rate of change of the dependent variable

zero. In other words, for our models, equilibrium
occurs when dN/dt = 0.

Stability: Imagine that the system is in equilibrium. We then disturb it a tiny amount and watch
to see what happens. If it returns to equilibrium directly, the system is called Stable. If
it continues to diverge from equilibrium, the
system is called Unstable. If the system does
neither, but rather just stays where it is disturbed to, the system is called Neutral or Meta-
stable.

Physical example: Consider a long, slender rod with a mass
at one end, and pivoted at the other. There are two equilibrium points, one with the mass above the pivot, the other
with the mass below. Clearly, if the first case is disturbed a tiny bit, it does not return. Rather, gravity
tends to make it continue to diverge. However, the second
case, if disturbed slightly, tends to return to the equilibrium point. Note that this case illustrates an oscillatory stability if there is some friction in the pivot, and
an oscillatory metastability if there is no friction.

An important point to learn from this example is that
we do not tend to encounter in nature systems at their unstable equilibrium points.

Stability Analysis of the Logistic Equation: As in any
stability analysis, the first step is to locate the equilibrium point or points. To do so, set

$$\frac{dN}{dt} = r_0 N(1 - N/K) = 0.$$

Recalling that r_0 and K are constants, this has two solutions, N = 0 and N = K. We proceed now to check the stability of the point N = K. To do so, we first introduce a
new dependent variable x, whose origin is at the point N =
K. Let N = K(1 + x), and substitute into the Logistic D.E.
to get

$$\frac{dx}{dt} = -r_0 x(1 + x) = -r_0 x - r_0 x^2.$$

This equation is really still exactly the same as the Logistic, which is to say, it is still Non-linear. We want to know whether tiny disturbances die away or grow. But since our interest is only in cases with $|x| \ll 1$, it follows that $|x| \gg |x^2| \gg |x^3| \gg \ldots$ and hence we approximate the D.E. for $x(t)$ by deleting all terms beyond the linear one. This operation is quite logically called linearization. Upon linearizing, our D.E. becomes

$$\frac{dx}{dt} = -r_0 x \qquad : |x| \ll 1.$$

Except for the minus sign, this is precisely the D.E. solved in Case 1. Thus

$$x(t) = x_0 \exp\{-r_0 t\},$$

where $x(0) = x_0$. In other words, x_0 is the size of the initial disturbance. Since $r_0 > 0$ for the Logistic Equation, the exponential tends to die away, and $x(t) \to 0$ as $t \to \infty$. This means that the population has a stable equilibrium at population size $N = K$, hence we would expect to find the population at this point.

We could repeat this procedure to determine the stability of the equilibrium at $N = 0$. If we make the substitution $N = Ky$ in the Logistic D.E. and linearize, we again arrive at the D.E. solved in Case 1. This time the RHS carries a plus sign, so we have a growing exponential solution. In other words, the equilibrium at $N = 0$ is unstable.

Notice that the consequences of the Stability Analysis are about the same as the observations which we were able to make viewing only the asymptotic nature of the complete solution. Specifically, if the population is very small, it initially grows (away from the unstable equilibrium point at $N = 0$) in an exponential fashion. Once N is no longer very small, our approximate solution found in doing

the Stability Analysis is no longer valid, because linearization is no longer representative. Also, since there is
only one stable equilibrium point, we would expect to find
the population (size) at that point, regardless of what its
size may have been in the past.

It is important to realize that when we discover an
unstable equilibrium point by having a locally exponentially growing solution, the solution invariably loses accuracy
as the system diverges from the equilibrium point. This is
because the linearization which led to the exponential solution ceases to be representative of the evolution of the
system once the dependent variable is not very small.

It is probably valuable at this point to repeat the
Stability Analysis of the Logistic D.E. once more, this
time graphically. We begin by plotting dN/dt against N.

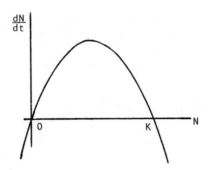

Recall that the equilibrium points occur when dN/dt = 0.
It is clear from the graph that this happens at the points
N = 0 and N = K.

To analyze the stability of the equilibrium at N = K
in a fashion analogous to the one employed in the mathematical description of Stability Analysis, we next constuct
a new set of co-ordinate axes with their origin at the
point (K,0) in the above figure, and redraw the portion of

the graph which is nearby:

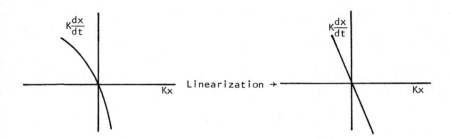

The operation of linearization has been represented in the figures. Notice that the curve (parabola) in the figure on the left has been replaced by the straight line whose slope equals the slope of the parabola at the origin (i.e. the tangent to the parabola at the origin).

It is now straightforward to see that these figures illustrate a stable equilibrium point. (For graphical purposes, the linearization is unnecessary - for mathematical analysis it is essential.) For example, imagine that the population is disturbed a tiny bit from the equilibrium point at $x = 0$ to say $x = x_0 > 0$. It is clear from either of the figures that at this population size, $dx/dt < 0$, hence the population tends to decrease in size as time passes. It is simple to repeat the argument for a small disturbance $x = x_0 < 0$, for which $dx/dt > 0$. These observations are sufficient to verify that the point $N = K$ (which is the same as $x = 0$) is an equilibrium point which is stable to small disturbances.

Problems

1. A population which initially numbers N_0 grows at a rate which is independent of the number of animals present and of time.

a. Write down a D.E. for the growth of the population.
b. Solve the D.E. which you wrote down.

2. A population grows according to the D.E.:

$$\frac{dN}{dt} = r_0 N.$$

Determine how long it takes the population to exactly double in size, assuming that $r_0 > 0$.

3. A population grows according to the D.E.:

$$\frac{dN}{dt} = r_0 (N-M)(K-N)/K$$

where r_0, M and K are positive constants, with M<<K.

a. Draw a sketch of $\frac{dN}{dt}$ versus N (Make sure you include the interval from N=0 to N>K.)
b. Determine the equilibrium population size(s).
c. Investigate the stability of each equilibrium point by using perturbation analysis. Do the results agree with what you can learn from the graph in part a?
d. Find the population size when the population growth rate is a maximum.
e. Find the complete solution analytically (hard).

4. A population grows according to the D.E.:

$$\frac{dN}{dt} = 1 - \exp\{-r_0(1-N/K)\}$$

where r_0 and K are positive constants.
a. Determine the equilibrium population size
b. Decide whether the equilibrium is stable, unstable or neutral.

References

The material contained in this section is so basic to population modeling that it can be found in virtually any text on the subject. Some useful references are:

Lotka, A.J., Elements of Mathematical Biology, Dover Publications, New York, 1956.

> Chapter 7 deals with exponential and logistic population growth, and includes a discussion of the fitting of models to real data. This book, which was originally published in 1924 with the title Elements of Physical Biology, is one of the classical references in the field on mathematical biology.

Wilson, E.O. and W.H. Bossert, A Primer of Population Biology, Sinauer Associates, Stamford, CT, 1971.

> Chapter 3 (pp. 92-111) provides a particularly simple and lucid development of the exponential and logistic models.

2 Stochastic Birth and Death Processes

In this section we will study two models for the growth of a single species population. We will recognize that in nature, births and deaths do not occur with clockwork precision, but rather happen probabilistically. Although this will complicate the mathematics considerably, one added aspect of reality will become available. Specifically, we will be able always to deal with integer numbers of organisms, thus avoiding the limitations inherent to models in which population size is treated as a continuous variable.

THE PURE BIRTH PROCESS

We begin with the simplest possible model which is at all realistic. For purposes of visualization, imagine that our population is composed of single cell animals which reproduce by cell division. Begin by making some assumptions:

1. All organisms are biologically identical and have cell division probabilities which do not depend upon time or population size.
2. The probability that an organism will divide into two organisms is independent of the past

history of the organism. In other words,
there is no maturation time.
3. The population is closed to migration both
in and out.

The independent variable is time t, which will be treated
as a continuous variable. Also, let:

$N(t)$ = the number of organisms present at time
t. Note that this is a non-negative,
integer valued random variable.

$p_N(t)$ = the probability that the population
numbers N at time t.

$\lambda\Delta t$ = the probability that an organism will
divide into two during the small inter-
val of time Δt. Note that λ is the
probabilistic analog of b, the intrin-
sic birth rate.

We would now like to determine $p_N(t+\Delta t)$. To do so, we
must recognize that two mutually exclusive situations at
time t can lead to this.

i. At time t, the population numbers N-1 with
probability $p_{N-1}(t)$ and one of the N-1 cells
divides with probability $(N-1)\lambda\Delta t$. Note that
by insisting that Δt is small, we can ignore
the case of more than one cell dividing.

ii. At time t, the population numbers N with
probability $p_N(t)$ and none of the N cells divides. This occurs with probability $(1 -
N\lambda\ \Delta t)$.

It therefore follows that

$$p_N(t+\Delta t) = p_{N-1}(t)\ (N-1)\ \lambda\ \Delta t + p_N(t)\ (1 - N\lambda\ \Delta t).$$

Next, rearrange and let $\Delta t \to 0$ to yield

$$\frac{dp_N(t)}{dt} = -\lambda N p_N(t) + \lambda(N-1)p_{N-1}(t).$$

-14-

This is called a Differential-Difference Equation. Its solution tells the probability that the population numbers N at time t, for all values of N. As with any differential equation of the first order, one initial condition is required. We will assume that at time t = 0 a census is taken and the population is found to number N(0) = j > 0. Thus,

$$\begin{cases} p_j(0) = 1 \\ p_N(0) = 0, \ N \neq j. \end{cases}$$

Note further that since the population can only grow larger it follows that for all t $\geq$ 0

$$p_N(t) = 0, \ N = 0,1,2,\ldots,j-1.$$

These observations allow us to solve the Differential-Difference Equation recursively. To do so, first let N = j to get

$$\frac{dp_j(t)}{dt} = -\lambda j p_j(t).$$

Recognize that this is identical to the D.E. which we solved while studying the simple deterministic single species population growth model. By separating variables and integrating, using $p_j(0) = 1$ we get

$$p_j(t) = \exp\{-\lambda jt\}.$$

This tells us that as time passes, the probability that the population numbers exactly j decays exponentially. But we are now in a position to find $p_{j+1}(t)$. To do so, set N = j+1 in the D-ΔE to get

$$\frac{dp_{j+1}(t)}{dt} + \lambda(j+1)p_{j+1}(t) = \lambda j p_j(t).$$

But the quantity $p_j(t)$ is known from above to be $\exp\{-\lambda jt\}$. In order to solve the resulting D.E., observe that if both sides of the equation are multiplied by $\exp\{\lambda(j+1)t\}$ (called an integrating factor) then the resulting equation can be integrated formally since the LHS is the derivative of a product. The result is

$$\exp\{\lambda(j+1)t\}p_{j+1}(t) = j \exp\{\lambda jt\} + \text{constant}.$$

In order to evaluate the constant of integration, we recall that $p_{j+1}(0) = 0$; thus the constant is $-j$, and so

$$p_{j+1}(t) = j \exp\{-\lambda jt\} (1 - \exp\{-\lambda t\}).$$

Next we would like to find $p_{j+2}(t)$. To do so, set N = j+2 in the D-ΔE. But the equation which results can be solved by exactly the same procedure as was employed to find $p_{j+1}(t)$. The result is

$$P_{j+2}(t) = \frac{(j+1)j}{2} \exp\{-\lambda jt\} (1 - \exp\{-\lambda t\})^2.$$

It should by now be obvious that for N = j, j+1, j+2,...

$$p_N(t) = \binom{N-1}{j-1} \exp\{-\lambda jt\} (1 - \exp\{-\lambda t\})^{N-j}.$$

It is easily verified that this is correct by induction using the D-ΔE.

So now we know $p_N(t)$. But that is not what we would really like to know. It would be much more interesting to determine the expected population size and the variance of the population size as functions of time. We proceed now to do this. To save a little writing, define

$$p = \exp\{-\lambda t\}$$

then

$$p_N(t) = \binom{N-1}{j-1} p^j (1-p)^{N-j}.$$

Note that in this form it is obvious that $p_{N+1}(t)$ is just p times a Binomial Distribution with parameters N and p.

The expected population size at time t is now found to be

$$E(N) = \sum_{i=j}^{\infty} ip_i(t) = p^j \sum_{k=0}^{\infty} (j+k) \binom{j+k-1}{k} (1-p)^k$$

which yields

$$E(N) = j \exp\{\lambda t\} \quad \left[\xrightarrow{\;\;\;} \quad N(t) = N_0 \exp\{r_0 t\}\right].$$

-16-

Recalling that the initial population size is j and
that λ is the probabilistic analog of the intrinsic birth
rate b makes it apparent that the expected population size
for the pure birth process is the same as the population
size for the deterministic analog with intrinsic death rate
equal to zero.

Although at first it might seem disappointing that all
the extra work was in vain, a little reflection illustrates
that this implies that the far simpler deterministic formulation leads to the correct answer on the average. There
is an even more reassuring observation available if we find
the variance of the population size as a function of time.

The variance of the population size at time t is

$$V(N) = E(N^2) - E(N)^2 = \sum_{i=j}^{\infty} i^2 p_i(t) - j^2 \exp\{2\lambda t\},$$

which yields

$$V(N) = j \exp\{\lambda t\} (\exp\{\lambda t\} - 1).$$

Note that this expression says that the variance of the
population size grows as time passes. This should come as
no surprise.

In order to assess the usefulness of the deterministic
version of the model for predicting future population size,
we need to know which increases faster, the standard deviation of the population size (i.e. the square root of the
variance) or the expected value of the population size. To
do so, we calculate the Coefficient of Variation, C.V.

$$C.V. = \frac{\sqrt{V(N)}}{E(N)} = j^{-\frac{1}{2}} (1 - \exp\{-\lambda t\})^{\frac{1}{2}} \sim j^{-\frac{1}{2}} \text{ as } t \to \infty.$$

This tells us that even as time $t \to \infty$, the variance remains
small when compared to the expected population size, so
long as j (the initial population size, which we called N_0
in the deterministic analog) is large. This of course is
just a reconfirmation of our earlier argument that the population must be large in our model.

THE BIRTH AND DEATH PROCESS

The Pure Birth Process considered above completely ig-
nored the very real possibility that organisms in the population could die without dividing. We next improve our
model by allowing for stochastic deaths. In return for the
added complexity, it now becomes more realistic to envision
our model as pertaining to any simple single species population, growing in an unlimited environment. The idea of
cell division may be replaced by ordinary births, with the
provision that births occur one at a time (i.e. no twins,
triplets,...) and that "mothers" survive childbearing. We
have thus implicitly created the following assumptions:

1. All individuals are biologically identical
   and have birth and death probabilities which
   do not depend upon time or population size.

2. The probability that an individual will give
   birth or die is independent of the past history for the individual. This does away with
   sex and age.

3. The population is closed to migration both in
   and out.

The variables are exactly the same as for the Pure
Birth Process with just one addition. Let

> $\mu \, \Delta t$ = the probability that an individual dies
> during the small interval of time Δt.
> Note that μ is the probabilistic analog of
> d, the intrinsic death rate.

Note that this model is also a close analog of the simple
single species deterministic growth model.

We proceed now to determine $p_N(t+\Delta t)$. Following the
arguments which we made while considering the Pure Birth
Process, we observe that any of three mutually exclusive
situations could lead to a population of size N at time
$t+\Delta t$.

-18-

1. At time t, the population numbered N-1 and a birth occurred during the next interval, Δt.
2. At time t, the population numbered N+1 and a death occurred during the next interval, Δt.
3. At time t, the population numbered N, and neither a birth nor a death occurred during the next interval, Δt.

Note that by assuming that Δt is small, we may ignore the possibility of multiple events.

This leads as before to the equation

$$p_N(t+\Delta t) = p_{N-1}(t)\lambda(N-1)\,\Delta t + p_N(t)\,(1-N\lambda\Delta t-N\mu\Delta t)$$
$$+ p_{N+1}(t)\mu(N+1)\Delta t.$$

Next, rearrange and let $\Delta t \to 0$, thus

$$\frac{dp_N(t)}{dt} = -N(\lambda+\mu)p_N(t) + \lambda(N-1)p_{N-1}(t)$$
$$+ \mu(N+1)p_{N+1}(t).$$

This is a D-ΔE for the population size density as a function of time. Instead of trying to solve this directly (recall that the solution of the D-ΔE for the Pure Birth Process was long, and the result was not too interesting) we proceed directly to finding $E(N)$ and $V(N)$. Note that this method can be used with the Pure Birth Process too.

Recall that by definition

$$E(N) = \sum_{i=0}^{\infty} ip_i(t).$$

Note that the sum runs over all possible population sizes. Although we will assume the population initially numbers j at t = 0, so that $E(N) = j$ at t = 0, since deaths can occur as well as births, the possibility of a population size smaller than j at times t > 0 does not vanish.

We now differentiate the definition of $E(N)$ with respect to time:

-19-

$$\frac{dE(N)}{dt} = \sum_{i=1}^{\infty} i \frac{dp_i(t)}{dt}$$

and use the D-ΔE to write (n.b. simplify notation: $p_N(t) = p_N$)

$$\frac{dE(N)}{dt} = \sum_{i=1}^{\infty} \{-(\lambda+\mu)i^2 p_i + \lambda i(i-1)p_{i-1}$$

$$+ \mu i(i+1)p_{i+1}\}$$

$$= \lambda \sum_{i=1}^{\infty} (-i^2 p_i + i^2 p_{i-1} - ip_{i-1})$$

$$- \mu \sum_{i=1}^{\infty} (i^2 p_i - i^2 p_{i+1} - ip_{i+1})$$

and by redefining the indices in the summations,

$$\frac{dE(N)}{dt} = \lambda \sum_{k=0}^{\infty} p_k \{-k^2 + (k+1)^2 - (k+1)\}$$

$$- \mu \sum_{k=0}^{\infty} p_k \{k^2 - (k-1)^2 - (k-1)\}$$

$$= \lambda \sum_{k=0}^{\infty} kp_k - \mu \sum_{k=0}^{\infty} kp_k = (\lambda-\mu)E(N).$$

It therefore follows that we must solve:

$$\frac{dE(N)}{dt} = (\lambda-\mu) E(N) : E(N) = j \text{ when } t = 0.$$

But this is the same D.E. that we have solved several times by separation of variables and integration. The solution is

$$E(N) = j \exp\{(\lambda-\mu)t\} \underset{\longrightarrow}{\longleftarrow} \left[N(t) = N_0 \exp\{r_0 t\}\right].$$

Note that if we replace j by N_0, λ by b, and μ by d, the solution is the same as for the determinstic, single species model.

We proceed in an analogous manner to find V(N). Recall

$$V(N) = E(N^2) - E(N)^2$$

where

$$E(N^2) = \sum_{i=1}^{\infty} i^2 p_i(t).$$

Differentiating both sides of the definition of $E(N^2)$ with respect to time, and then using the D-ΔE leads to

$$\frac{dE(N^2)}{dt} + 2(\mu-\lambda) \ E(N^2) = (\lambda+\mu)j \ \exp\{(\lambda-\mu)t\}.$$

As with the higher order equations of the Pure Birth Process, this D.E. can be solved by means of an integrating factor. It is clear from the form of the left-hand side that the appropriate choice is $\exp\{2(\mu-\lambda)t\}$. It follows that

$$\exp\{2(\mu-\lambda)t\} \ E(N^2)$$
$$= j(\lambda+\mu) \int \exp\{(\lambda-\mu)t\}\exp\{2(\mu-\lambda)t\}dt$$
$$= - \frac{j(\lambda+\mu)}{\lambda-\mu} \exp\{(\mu-\lambda)t\} + \text{constant}.$$

To evaluate the constant of integration, observe that $V(N) = 0$ at $t = 0$ (since the population size is known exactly). Thus use

$$E(N^2) = E(N)^2 \text{ at } t = 0.$$

Following a bit of algebra, we arrive at

$$V(N) = \frac{j(\lambda+\mu)}{\lambda-\mu} \exp\{(\lambda-\mu)t\}(\exp\{(\lambda-\mu)t\} - 1).$$

Note that the variance depends not only on the difference between λ and μ (the intrinsic rate of growth) but also on their sum. This should actually come as no great surprise. Clearly, the larger the vital rates, the faster the population will grow away from its known initial size.

There is one more topic related to the Birth and Death Process which is too interesting to omit, but which requires the development of too much mathematics to do completely. What we would like to determine is the probability that a population which initially numbers j will become extinct. To do this, we must solve the D-ΔE. The difficulty is that this is not ordinarily done by the laborious method employed for the Pure Birth Process. Instead, we would write down a Partial Differential Equation for the Moment Generating Function for the probability distribution for the population size as a function of time. We would then solve, only to discover that the only case for which we could easily write down $p_0(t)$ (the extinction probability at time t) is the one in which the initial population size $j = 1$. The result would be:

$$p_0(t|j=1) = \frac{\mu \exp\{(\lambda-\mu)t\} - \mu}{\lambda \exp\{(\lambda-\mu)t\} - \mu}.$$

But then recognize that if a population starts with j individuals, if it is to become extinct, each of the j lines of descent must die out independently. Thus

$$p_0(t|j) = \{p_0(t|j=1)\}^j = \left\{\frac{\mu \exp\{(\lambda-\mu)t\} - \mu}{\lambda \exp\{(\lambda-\mu)t\} - \mu}\right\}^j.$$

To find the probability of ultimate extinction, we must let $t \to \infty$ in $p_0(t|j)$.

Three distinct cases exist:

$\underline{\lambda \le \mu}$: Clearly, as $t \to \infty$, the exponentials die out, so

$\lim\limits_{t\to\infty} p_0(t|j) = 1$ (i.e. extinction certain).

$\underline{\lambda > \mu}$: Clearly, as $t \to \infty$, the exponentials dominate, so

$\lim\limits_{t\to\infty} p_0(t|j) = \left\{\frac{\mu}{\lambda}\right\}^j$ (i.e. extinction may occur, but is not certain).

$\underline{\lambda = \mu}$: This time, we must expand the exponentials in form of series to evaluate the limit. The result is

$\lim\limits_{t\to\infty} p_0(t|j) = 1$ (i.e. extinction certain, even though $E(N)$ remains at j).

1. Given that $p_{j+2}(0) = 0$, solve the D.E.:

$$\frac{dp_{j+2}(t)}{dt} + \lambda(j+2)p_{j+2}(t)$$

$$= \lambda(j+1)j\exp\{-\lambda jt\}(1 - \exp\{-\lambda t\}).$$

2. Prove by induction using the D-ΔE for the Pure Birth Process

$$p_N(t) = \binom{N-1}{j-1} \exp\{-\lambda jt\}(1 - \exp\{-\lambda t\})^{N-j}.$$

3. Find $E(N)$ and $V(N)$ for the Pure Birth Process
    a. From the definitions of the expectation and variance in terms of the probability density (given in problem 2 above).
    b. Directly from the D-ΔE, without ever finding $p_N(t)$.

4. Find $V(N)$ for the Birth and Death Process, starting with the definitions: $V(N) = E(N^2) - E(N)^2$, where $V(N) = 0$ at $t = 0$

$$E(N^2) = \sum_{i=1}^{\infty} i^2 p_i(t)$$

$$E(N) = j \exp\{(\lambda-\mu)t\}$$

$$\frac{dp_N(t)}{dt} = -N(\lambda+\mu)p_N(t) + \lambda(N-1)p_{N-1}(t)$$

$$+ \mu(N+1)p_{N+1}(t).$$

5. Determine what happens to $E(N)$ and $V(N)$ for the Birth and Death Process if $\lambda = \mu$. Start from the expression for $E(N)$ given in problem 4, and the expression for $V(N)$ which you found in solving problem 4.

References

The material in this section can be found in virtually any text on stochastic processes. Two useful references are:

Bailey, N.T.J., <u>The Elements of Stochastic Processes</u>, John
Wiley and Sons, New York, 1964.

Chapter 8 contains a thorough but rather terse treatment of stochastic birth and death models. Much of
the mathematical detail is left to the reader.

Pielou, E.C., <u>An Introduction to Mathematical Ecology</u>,
Wiley-Interscience, New York, 1969.

Chapter 1 provides a biologically motivated development of stochastic birth and death models. The treatment in this book seems particularly clear.

3 A Two Age Group Population Model

We proceed next to develop a mathematical model for the growth of a population in which newborn animals do not become fertile until a period of time has passed. This situation is rather realistic for many species, including humans. In return for the added realism of the model, certain complications will necessarily arise.

We begin by making several simplifying assumptions:

1. The only individuals in the population who are counted are the females. Males are present in sufficient numbers to provide for reproduction.
2. All females in a given age group (cohort) exhibit the same fertility and mortality.
3. The population is closed to migration, both in and out.
4. The females in one age group are the children of the females in the previous age group. In other words, successive cohorts are separated by a generation.

5. Females only remain fertile for one generation (unit of time). After this time (post-menopause) females need not die, but are no longer counted in the model.

The independent variable is time t, which may take on only non-negative integer values corresponding to successive generations. Also, let:

B_t = the number of females (babies) in the cohort which have not yet reached reproductive maturity at time t.

A_t = the number of females (adults) in the cohort which are presently in the reproductive years at time t.

ℓ = the fraction of the younger cohort which survives to reproductive maturity.

m = the average number of daughters born to a female during the reproductive years.

The mathematical model is easily seen to consist of just two equations. The first equation recognizes that the number of babies in generation t is just m times the number of adults in generation t. The second equation recognizes that the number of adults in generation t is just ℓ times the number of babies in generation t - 1. Thus

$$\left. \begin{array}{l} B_t = mA_t \\ A_t = \ell B_{t-1} \end{array} \right\} : t = 1, 2, 3, \ldots$$

Comments: 1. As is typical of such population models, it is possible for B_t and A_t to assume non-integer values. Thus results are approximated to the nearest integer and populations are assumed to be large.

2. Must recognize that in general, m and ℓ are not constants, but rather depend upon time and population size. Specific functional representations constitute the hardest part

of the model to justify.

3. Assume the initial number of babies B_0 is known.

Case 1: As a first assumption, let $m = m_0$ and $\ell = \ell_0$, both constants.

Solve: $B_t = m_0 A_t$

$\qquad\qquad\qquad$: $t = 1, 2, 3, \ldots$ & B_0 known.

$A_t = \ell_0 B_{t-1}$

Method: First eliminate A_t between the two equations to get

$B_t = R_0 B_{t-1}$ where $R_0 = m_0 \ell_0$.

We identify this as a Linear Difference Equation.

Although a wide variety of techniques are available, the resulting equation is most easily solved by induction:

$$B_1 = R_0 B_0$$
$$B_2 = R_0 B_1 = R_0^2 B_0$$

$\cdot\ \cdot\ \cdot$

and in general $\quad B_t = R_0 B_{t-1} = \cdot\ \cdot\ \cdot = R_0^t B_0$

As a function of time in generations this looks like

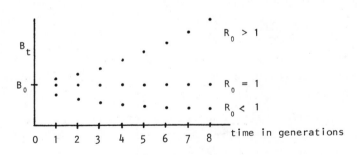

Case 2: As an improvement to the first case we will assume that women born in large cohorts have fewer children apiece than women born in small cohorts

-27-

(this appears to be the case at least for developed nations). For convenience, continue to assume that $\ell = \ell_0$, but let the maternity function decline linearly according to the relationship

$$m = m_0(1 - A_t/H) \quad : m_0, H \text{ positive constants.}$$

Substituting the assumed forms of m and ℓ into the governing equations, and eliminating A_t leads to:

Solve: $\quad B_t = R_0 B_{t-1} - \dfrac{R_0 \ell_0}{H} B_{t-1}^2 \quad : t = 1, 2, 3, \ldots$

$$B_0 \text{ known}, \quad R_0 = m_0 \ell_0.$$

Method: Unfortunately, this is a Non-linear Difference Equation. No general method exists for finding an exact solution.

Two procedures for extracting solutions will be investigated. The first is the method of Stability Analysis, the second is a graphical technique.

Stability Analysis: In order to decide if a Stability Analysis will yield any meaningful results, we must first decide if there are any equilibrium points.

Equilibrium: The population is in equilibrium if successive birth cohorts are the same size. Thus, set $B_t = B_{t-1} = B_e$ in the Difference Equation to yield

$$B_e = \frac{H(R_0 - 1)}{R_0 \ell_0}.$$

Note that there is a range of equilibrium population sizes depending upon the value of R_0, ℓ_0 and H. In order that B_e be positive (which we require on physical grounds) $R_0 > 1$.

Stability: Introduce a new dependent variable, x_t, with origin at $B_t = B_e$. Choose to let $B_t = B_e + x_t$, and substitute into the Non-linear Difference Equation to get

$$x_t = (2 - R_0)x_{t-1} - \frac{R_0 \ell_0}{H} x_{t-1}^2.$$

Next we demand that $|x_t| << B_e$, and linearize to get

$$x_t = (2 - R_0)x_{t-1}.$$

Identify this as a Linear Difference Equation. The solution follows directly from the same inductive procedure used to solve Case 1. If the initial small disturbance from equilibrium is x_0, then

$$x_t = x_0(2 - R_0)^t \ : \ R_0 > 1.$$

Interpreting the stability requires a bit of care. Clearly, the equilibrium is stable if $|2 - R_0| \leq 1$, and unstable otherwise. But, if $(2 - R_0) < 0$, x_t alternates in sign for successive values of t. As a function of the value of R_0 the stability looks like:

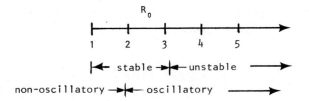

Probably the best way to understand the meaning of this result is to look at the exact graphical solution to the Nonlinear Difference Equation.

Graphical Solution: Sometimes it is possible to find an exact solution graphically, even when such a solution can not be found by analytic means. We will do this first for a value of R_0 on the interval (1,2). Recall that the stability analysis told us that the equilibrium associated with this range of R_0 was stable and non-oscillatory.

We begin by listing the equations to be solved:

$$B_t = m_0(1 - A_t/H)A_t$$
$$A_t = \ell_0 B_{t-1}$$

$: \ t = 1, 2, 3, \ldots$
B_0 known, $R_0 = m_0\ell_0$.

-29-

For convenience we will refer to the first of these as the
maternity equation, and the second as the survivorship
equation. Note that the maternity equation is a parabola
in (B,A) co-ordinates, and the survivorship equation is a
straight line. Both pass through the origin. For a particular value of R_0 on (1,2) these look as in the graph
on the left below:

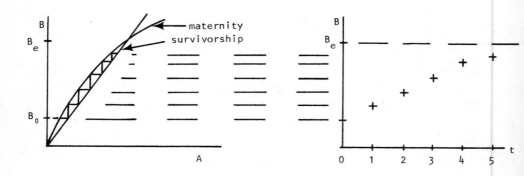

As illustrated, the graphical solution procedure consists of a projecting horizontally from B_0 until the survivorship line is met. This occurs at the point A_1. Next,
we project vertically from A_1 until the maternity line is
met. This occurs at B_1. The process is then repeated. To
illustrate the size of successive birth cohorts, the values
found on the left are projected over to the graph on the
right. Notice that even for an initial population size far
below B_e the successive birth cohorts approach B_e, and do
so without ever overshooting. (Successive over and under-
shooting would be identified as an oscillatory re-establish-
ment of equilibrium by a Stability Analysis.) It is important to note that the method of Stability Analysis is only
applicable for small disturbances from the equilibrium
point, while the Graphical Method is very general. It is
also worth noting at this point that the step of linearizing the equation in the Stability Analysis is equivalent to

-30-

replacing the maternity line by a straight line which is
tangent to the parabola at $B = B_e$, and passes through B_e.
This observation helps illustrate why the Stability Analysis is only valid for small excursions from B_e.

We proceed next to solve the governing equations for a
value of R_0 on the interval $(2,3)$. We employ the Graphical
Method exactly as above. Note that this time the maternity
line (parabola) reaches a maximum before intersecting the
survivorship line at $B = B_e$.

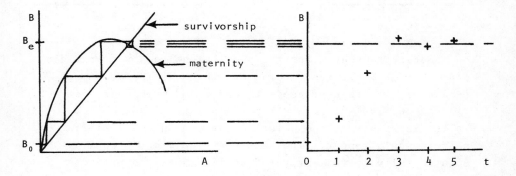

Notice that far below B_e the population grows rapidly,
but then overshoots the equilibrium point; it then proceeds
to close in on B_e by successively under and overshooting.
Thus for a small perturbation away from B_e one would expect
an oscillatory return to equilibrium (as predicted by the
Stability Analysis of the case.)

The third possible type of solution, as predicted by
the Stability Analysis, occurs when $R_0 > 3$. This case is
illustrated by the exact Graphical Solution below:

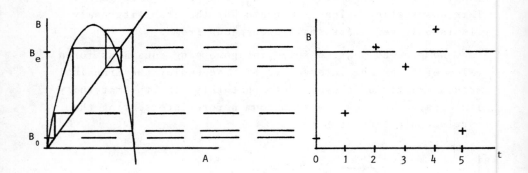

Notice that at first the population grows very rapidly from $B_0 \ll B_e$. It then overshoots the equilibrium population size. It then proceeds to under and overshoot, getting successively further from the point of equilibrium. It is clear that if the solution was continued, a similar pattern would repeat. The nature of the exact Graphical Solution illustrates why the Stability Analysis predicts an oscillatory instability for $R_0 > 3$.

We will consider this model in greater detail later.

Problems

1. Start with the difference equation:

    $$\frac{N(t+\Delta t) - N(t)}{\Delta t} = r_0 N(t).$$

    a. Find the solution $N(k\Delta t)$: k=0, 1, 2, . . . by induction, given that $N(0) = N_0$.

    b. In the original difference equation, let $\Delta t \to 0$ and solve the resulting differential equation again with $N(0) = N_0$.

    c. In your answer to part a, let $\Delta t \to 0$ and $k \to \infty$, such that $k\Delta t \to t$. The result should be an expression which defines the exponential function as a

-32-

limit. Compare the series expansion of the exponential and the limit so as to illustrate their equivalence.

2. Starting with the difference equation version of the Logistic Equation with $\Delta t = 1$, make the necessary change of variables to show that it is equivalent to the equation:

$$B_t = R_0 B_{t-1} - \frac{R_0 \ell_0}{H} B_{t-1}^2.$$

3. Consider the pair of equations:

$$\left. \begin{array}{l} B_t = m_0 A_t (1 - A_t/H) \\[2ex] A_t = \ell_0 B_{t-1} \end{array} \right\} \quad R_0 = m_0 \ell_0.$$

Linearize these equations around their equilibrium point and then repeat the graphical solution for R_0 on the intervals $(1,2)$, $(2,3)$ and $(3,\infty)$. Point out the difference between the graphical solutions to the linear and non-linear versions.

References

Although an analogous form of the two age group model appears in the economics literature, perhaps the most accessible simple exposition in a population context is to be found in the journal article:

Lee, R.D., "The Formal Dynamics of Controlled Populations and the Echo, the Boom and the Bust", Demography, Volume 11, Number 4, pp. 563-585, November, 1974.

The two age group model is discussed along with the method of graphical solution in section 2 of this paper. The paper then goes on to investigate a many age group model which is beyond the scope of the present discussion.

4 Time Delayed Logistic Equations

So far, we have assumed that our population has no effect upon the environment from which it gains its livelihood. This is really only reasonable if the population numbers are so small as not to influence the availability of resources. The Carrying Capacity of any environment, for example, depends upon the food supply which is available at any time, which in turn depends upon the recent history of the population size.

In order to assess the effect of finite resource regeneration time, we will study a modified form of the Logistic Equation

$$\frac{dN(t)}{dt} = r_0 N(t) \left[1 - \frac{N(t)}{K} \right] : r_0, K > 0, \text{ constant.}$$

Recall that the solution of this equation leads to the conclusion that the population is asymptotically stable with $N \sim K$ as $t \to \infty$.

We now modify that equation to include the idea that the intrinsic growth rate of the population is influenced by the size of the population at time T earlier. This is accomplished by modifying the equation so it reads

$$\frac{dN(t)}{dt} = r_0 N(t) \left[1 - \frac{N(t-T)}{K} \right].$$

While the meaning of this equation is quite clear, it is not very realistic, and happens to lead to a rather messy solution. We will therefore proceed to improve our assumption immediately. To do so, we replace the influence of the population <u>exactly</u> time T earlier by a term which reflects the influence of the population at all previous times. We want this term to reflect several rather realistic assumptions:

1. The population size in the distant past should have little effect on present growth.
2. The population size a very short time ago should also have little effect on present growth.
3. The main effect on the present growth should come from the population size T time units ago.

The desired improvement is achieved mathematically by replacing the term $N(t-T)$ by a weighted average of the form

$$\int_{-\infty}^{t} N(\tau) Q(t-\tau) d\tau$$

where to be consistent with the assumptions, $Q(t)$ appears as in the sketch, and

$$\int_{0}^{\infty} Q(\xi) d\xi = 1.$$

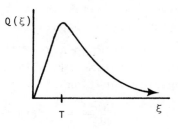

We will eventually have to specify the exact form for $Q(\xi)$ explicitly; however this is not necessary yet. Note that if we set $Q(\xi) = \delta(\xi-T)$, the Dirac Delta Function, then we would get back the equation with $N(t-T)$ in it.

The Model: The Time Delayed Logistic Differential Equation

$$\frac{dN(t)}{dt} = r_0 N(t) \left[1 - \frac{1}{K} \int_{-\infty}^{t} N(\tau)Q(t-\tau)d\tau \right]$$

$$: \int_{0}^{\infty} Q(\xi)d\xi = 1.$$

This is actually a non-linear integro-differential equation of the Volterra type, with a displacement kernel. We will not even attempt to find a solution directly. All we really wish to know are the stability properties of the equation.

Stability Analysis:

Equilibrium - dN/dt = 0 which implies that N = constant which, in turn, implies that N = K.

Stability - Let $N(t) = K\left[1 + x(t)\right]$.

Substitute into the equation and demand that $|x(t)| << 1$. This permits the resulting equation to be linearized to

$$\frac{dx(t)}{dt} = -r_0 \int_{-\infty}^{t} x(\tau)Q(t-\tau)d\tau.$$

At this point we would ordinarily proceed to find the Laplace Transform of the equation. While this is perfectly correct, a more transparent method of solution exists. Inspired by our previous success with exponential solutions to Logistic Equations, we assume that $x(t) = x_0\exp\{\lambda t\}$. Substituting leads to

$$x_0\lambda\exp\{\lambda t\} = -r_0 x_0 \int_{-\infty}^{t} \exp\{\lambda\tau\}Q(t-\tau)d\tau$$

which yields

$$\lambda = -r_0 \underbrace{\int_{0}^{\infty} \exp\{-\lambda\zeta\}Q(\zeta)d\zeta}_{\equiv \tilde{Q}(\lambda) \ : \ \text{the Laplace Transform of } Q(\xi).} \quad : \ \zeta = t - \tau$$

-37-

The resulting equation is called the Characteristic Equation, and is given by

$$\lambda + r_0 \tilde{Q}(\lambda) = 0.$$

Once the explicit form of $Q\{\xi\}$ is specified, the Characteristic Equation is used to determine λ. Note that x_0, the initial disturbance, does not appear. This is to be expected.

Digression - Before specifying an explicit form for $Q(\zeta)$, let us attempt to anticipate how to interpret the results. First, recognize that the solution to the Characteristic Equation will result in a (finite or infinite) set of roots, $\lambda_1, \lambda_2, \lambda_3, \ldots$. The solution to the linearized form of the equation is then of the form

$$x(t) = x_{01}\exp\{\lambda_1 t\} + x_{02}\exp\{\lambda_2 t\} + \ldots.$$

Clearly, if this is to represent a stable solution, every term in it must die out as $t \to \infty$. If any term blows-up, the solution is unstable. We must also realize that in general, the roots $\lambda_1, \lambda_2, \ldots$ will be complex numbers. We must therefore understand the nature of complex exponentials.

Consider $X = \exp\{Z\}$, where $Z = u + iv$, with $i = \sqrt{-1}$.

Then
$$X = \exp\{Z\} = \exp\{u+iv\} = \exp\{u\}\exp\{iv\}$$
$$= \exp\{u\}\left[1 + iv + (iv)^2/2! + (iv)^3/3! + (iv)^4/4! + \ldots\right]$$
$$= \exp\{u\}\left[\{1 - v^2/2! + v^4/4! - \ldots\} + i\{v - v^3/3! + v^5/5! + \ldots\}\right]$$
$$= \exp\{u\}\left[\cos v + i \sin v\right].$$

This identity is easily interpreted:

1. The growth of X is determined entirely by $\text{Re}\{Z\} = u$
    a. If $u > 0$, solution grows (unstable).
    b. If $u < 0$, solution shrinks (stable).

     c. If u = 0, solution remains fixed in
        size (neutral).
2. The periodicity of X is determined entirely
   by $Im\{Z\} = v$
     a. If v = 0, solution does not oscillate.
     b. If v ≠ 0, solution is oscillatory,
        with more rapid oscillation associ-
        ated with larger $|v|$.

A convenient way to exhibit Z is by means of a graph of the complex Z plane.

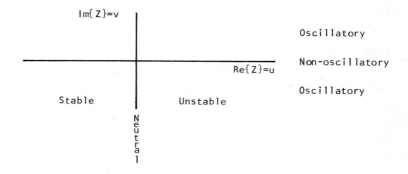

By plotting $Z = \lambda_1, \lambda_2, \lambda_3, \ldots$ in the complex plane, we can read off the stability of the equation directly.

We will next consider an explicit form for $Q\{\zeta\}$. The choice is dictated by a desire to produce results which are simple to interpret, and by the conditions stated earlier.

    1. $Q(\zeta) = 0$ for $\zeta = 0$ and $\zeta \to \infty$.
    2. $Q(\zeta)$ a maximum at $\zeta = T$.
    3. $\int_0^\infty Q(\zeta)\,d\zeta = 1$.

The form which we will choose is $Q(\zeta) = (\zeta/T^2)\exp\{-\zeta/T\}$. Taking the Laplace transform leads to $\tilde{Q}(\lambda) = 1/(1 + \lambda T)^2$,

which when substituted into the Characteristic Equation
yields

$$\lambda^3 + (2/T)\lambda^2 + (1/T^2)\lambda + (r_0/T^2) = 0.$$

This is a cubic equation, hence it has three roots whose
values determine the nature of the solution to the original
equation. If we could plot these roots in the complex λ
plane, we could then read off the stability. Unfortunately, unless we are willing to specify values for r_0 and T,
this is not possible. Note also that even if we did
specify values, we would then have to solve a cubic equation for its roots. Since we are only interested in knowing
whether the roots fall in the left or right half of the
complex λ plane, a method is available.

The Routh Array

In doing Stability Analyses we are regularly confronted
with the problem of deciding if any roots λ_j of a polynomial
$P(\lambda) = 0$ have $\text{Re}\{\lambda_j\} > 0$. Imagine that

$$P(\lambda) = a_0\lambda^n + a_1\lambda^{n-1} + a_2\lambda^{n-2} + \cdot \cdot \cdot + a_{n-1}\lambda$$

$$+ a_n = 0.$$

The number of roots that lie in the right half of the complex λ plane then equals the number of sign changes in the
first (left-hand) column of the following array.

$$
\begin{array}{cccc}
a_0 & a_2 & a_4 & a_6 \quad \cdot \cdot \cdot \\
a_1 & a_3 & a_5 & a_7 \quad \cdot \cdot \cdot \\
b_{1,1} & b_{1,2} & b_{1,3} & \cdot \cdot \cdot \\
b_{2,1} & b_{2,2} & b_{2,3} & \cdot \cdot \cdot \\
\end{array}
$$

where

$$b_{1,1} = \frac{\begin{vmatrix} a_0 & a_2 \\ a_1 & a_3 \end{vmatrix}}{-a_1}$$

$$b_{1,2} = \frac{\begin{vmatrix} a_0 & a_4 \\ a_1 & a_5 \end{vmatrix}}{-a_1}$$

$b_{n-2,1}$

$b_{n-1,1}$ and the same 2x2
pattern for successive $b_{i,j}$.

Comments:

1. Notice that there are $n+1$ terms in the first column.
2. If there is a zero term in the first column, replace it by ε. Then proceed through analysis as before. At the end, let $\varepsilon \to 0$.
3. If there is a zero row, this means that there is a purely imaginary root pair (i.e. $\lambda = \pm i\alpha$). To proceed, form auxiliary equation as follows:

   If the rth row is all zeros, go to $(r-1)^{st}$ row, whose elements are K_1, K_2, . . .

   Form
   $$K_1 \lambda^{n-r} + K_2 \lambda^{n-r-2} + K_3 \lambda^{n-r-4} + \ldots$$
   Then find $\frac{d}{d\lambda}$ and use coefficients to fill r^{th} row.

Example: $P(\lambda) = \lambda^5 + 5\lambda^4 - 15\lambda^3 - 125\lambda^2 - 226\lambda - 120 = 0$.

(N.B. Roots are $\lambda = -1, -2, -3, -4, +5$.
Thus there is one root in right half of λ plane.)

Routh Array

+1	-15	-226	
+5	-125	-120	Interpretation-
+10	-202	0	Since there is one sign change in the
-24	-120		first column of the
-252	0		Routh Array, there is
-120			one root with positive real part.

We return now to the consideration of the stability of the time delayed Logistic Equation. Recall that the Characteristic Equation for this problem with $Q(\zeta) = (\zeta/T^2)\exp(-\zeta/T)$ is given by

$$P(\lambda) = \lambda^3 + (2/T)\lambda^2 + (1/T^2)\lambda + (r_0/T^2) = 0.$$

It is not hard to show by means of the Routh Array that for a cubic polynomial of the form

$$P(\lambda) = \lambda^3 + a\lambda^2 + b\lambda + c = 0$$

the conditions for all of the roots to have negative real parts are

1. $a > 0$, $c > 0$
2. $ab > c$.

In terms of the quantities in the Characteristic Equation, this corresponds with

1. $T > 0$, $r_0 > 0$
2. $r_0 T < 2$.

Clearly, from the problem statement, r_0 and T are positive on physical grounds. Thus for stability we need only have $r_0 T < 2$. In other words, the larger the value of the growth rate constant r_0, the smaller the modal time delay T must be to avoid destabilizing the system.

There is another way to conceptualize results. First, observe that $1/r_0 = T_*$ may be viewed as the characteristic growth time for the population. (T_* is the time between successive births to any individual in the population in the limit as $N \to 0$.) The stability condition then reads $T < 2T_*$.

There is one further question that we can ask about the above model. Within the stable region, is the behavior oscillatory or non-oscillatory? To answer this question, we must know whether the three roots of the Characteristic Equation are all purely real (non-oscillatory), or is one real and the other two a complex conjugate pair (oscillatory). Note that for a cubic equation, these are the only possibilities. Since the Characteristic Equation is cubic, we can employ Cardano's Method.

<u>Cardano's Method</u> (actually, only as much of it as we need)

Given: $P(\lambda) = \lambda^3 + a\lambda^2 + b\lambda + c = 0$.

Define: $A = (3b - a^2)/3$ and $B = (2a^2 - 9ab + 27c)/27$.

Then the roots of $P(\lambda) = 0$ are purely real and different if and only if

$$\frac{A^3}{27} + \frac{B^2}{4} < 0.$$

(N.B.   Cardano's Method goes on to give
        formulas for actually finding the
        roots - messy!)

For the Characteristic Equation under consideration, the resulting condition for non-oscillatory stability is

$$0 < r_0 T < \frac{4}{27} \approx 0.15.$$

Thus the solution is oscillatory and stable if

$$\frac{4}{27} < r_0 T < 2.$$

One thing we have not yet considered is what happens if the system is unstable (and oscillatory as found above). But since we have been looking at a linearized analysis, we do not have the right to ask (the equations). We therefore leave this question until later.

Another thing we have not asked is whether the above results are peculiar to our choice of $Q(\zeta)$. We would of course hope that they are general in spirit if not in detail. To assess this we must solve for other choices of $Q(\zeta)$. The only one we will look at in any detail is the one which leads to the time lag of exactly T.

As noted earlier, the choice $Q(\zeta) = \delta(\zeta - T)$ leads to the time lag of exactly T in the resource regulation term of the Logistic Equation.

The Laplace Transform of $Q(\zeta)$ is easily seen to be

$\tilde{Q}(\lambda) = \exp\{-\lambda T\}$. The Characteristic Equation is therefore given by

$$\lambda + r_0 \exp\{-\lambda T\} = 0.$$

But since this is a transcendental equation instead of a polynomial equation, the method for locating the roots is different. We will sketch this out, skipping over some non-trivial details.

We first consider the conditions for stability which is of course that no root of the Characteristic Equation have $\mathrm{Re}\{\lambda\} > 0$. (Note that the Characteristic Equation has an infinite number of roots.) We will do this as follows. Recognize that the boundary between stability and instability occurs as the root with the largest real part passes through $\mathrm{Re}\{\lambda\} = 0$. We therefore set $\lambda = i\beta$ in the Characteristic Equation. Splitting the complex equation which results into real and imaginary parts yields

$$r_0 \cos(\beta T) = 0$$
$$\beta - r_0 \sin(\beta T) = 0.$$

The first equation is satisfied if $\beta T = \pi/2$. The second equation then provides the condition for stability

$$0 < r_0 T < \pi/2 \simeq 1.57.$$

Next, we split the stable region into two parts, one corresponding to non-oscillatory stability, the other to oscillatory stability. To do so we seek the condition that causes the dominant root (the one with the largest real part) to be purely real. Thus we set $\lambda = -\alpha/T$ in the Characteristic Equation. This provides

$$\alpha \exp\{-\alpha\} = r_0 T.$$

It is not hard to see that $r_0 T$ assumes its largest value when $\alpha = 1$, thus the condition for non-oscillatory stability is

$$0 < r_0 T < \exp\{-1\} \simeq 0.37.$$

Thus the solution is oscillatory and stable if

$$\exp\{-1\} < r_0 T < \pi/2.$$

Perhaps the most important thing to notice about the above two sets of results for the concentrated and smeared-out time delays is that, though formally quite different, both lead to rather similar results. Specifically, so long as the time delay is no greater than about the order of the characteristic growth time (T_*) for the population, the growth process is stable. Long time delays lead to instability. Further, these results carry over to other choices of $Q(\zeta)$ which satisfy our rather loose conditions on shape and size.

Problems

1. Given that $Q(\zeta) = (\zeta/T^2)\exp\{-\zeta/T\}$

   a. Show that $Q(\zeta)$ has a maximum at $\zeta = T$.
   b. Find the Laplace Transform of $Q(\zeta)$ by direct integration.

2. Given the equation $P(\lambda) = \lambda^3 + a\lambda^2 + b\lambda + c = 0$, use the Routh Array to determine the conditions for all of the roots of the equation to have negative real parts.

3. Decide how many of the roots lie in the right half of the complex λ plane for the polynomial equation

   $$P(\lambda) = \lambda^5 - 3\lambda^4 - 23\lambda^3 - 33\lambda^2 + 166\lambda + 120 = 0.$$

4. Consider the discrete time growth equation

   $$\frac{N(t+\Delta t) - N(t)}{\Delta t} = r(N) N(t).$$

   Assume that the intrinsic growth rate $r(N)$ includes a resource recovery time of one time interval, and is logistic in nature; thus let

   $$r(N) = r_0 \left[1 - \frac{N(t-\Delta t)}{K} \right].$$

a. Determine the stability of the equilibrium at
   N = K. For convenience, let Δt = T.
b. Make a plot of the root(s) of the Characteristic
   Equation in the complex plane, clearly illustrat-
   ing the regions of stability and instability.
c. Compare the results of the above model with those
   found earlier for the discrete time logistic
   equation without explicit time delays. Also, list
   the results for the continuous time logistic equations with time delays which have been studied.

References

The model discussed in this section has been studied
at length by R.M. May. The material on the meaning of the
location of the roots of the Characteristic Equation in
the complex plane can be found in any introductory text on
differential equations.

May, R.M., Stability and Complexity in Model Ecosystems,
Princeton University Press, Princeton, NJ, 1973.

On pages 94-100 the ideas of time delays are discussed
in biological terms, but most of the mathematics is
absent. A thorough treatment of the material in this
section can be found in the following paper in the
technical literature.

May, R.M., "Time-Delay versus Stability in Population
Models with Two and Three Trophic Levels", Ecology,
Volume 54, pp. 315-325, 1973.

Most of the mathematics of interest can be found in
section ii of the appendix of this paper.

5 Population Growth in a Time-Varying Environment

The ability of a population of animals to grow depends intimately upon the nature of the environment from which the animals gain their livelihood. If the availability of environmental resources varies with time (as opposed to population numbers) this may have some unexpected effects upon the growth process. Unfortunately, the mathematical characterizations of many realistic sorts of fluctuations are very difficult; even some conceptually simple models lead to results which are still disputed by biological researchers. To gain some insight, let us look at the simplest possible model, and see what can be learned.

Without repeating the arguments which lead to the first case studied under the heading "Two Age Group Models" we simply write down a structurally identical model (with one exception)

$$N_t = R_t N_{t-1} : \quad t = 1, 2, 3, \ldots ; N_0 \text{ known.}$$

Here, N_t is the population size in generation t, which is seen to depend upon the population size one generation

earlier through a multiplicative growth factor R_t. In the
earlier model, R_t was assumed to be a constant, called R_0;
now it is taken to be a random variable, drawn from a sta-
tionary (i.e. time independent) probability density function $f(R)$. For future reference, we will assume the
density $f(R)$ has mean ρ and standard deviation σ.

The population size as a function of generation number
is easily found as it was for the simpler model with R_t =
R_0 by induction. The result is

$$N_t = N_0 \prod_{j=1}^{t} R_j .$$

The next question we might reasonably think of to ask
is, what is the expected population size after t generations? If the R_t are independent of one another

$$E(N_t) = N_0 \; E\left[\prod_{j=1}^{t} R_j\right] = N_0 \; E(R)^t = N_0 \rho^t ,$$

where it will be recalled that ρ is the arithmetic mean of
the random variable R. Notice that the future development
is entirely determined by whether $\rho > 0$ or $\rho < 0$. The first
case leads to unbounded growth, the second to asymptotic
extinction.

The trouble with this approach is that, although it
gives a correct picture of the expected population size, it
may give a completely erroneous picture of nearly every
population. The truthfulness of the picture given by the
expected population size is dependent upon the variance of
R, but that is getting ahead of ourselves. We proceed more
carefully.

As an example of the potential inadequacy of the expected value to characterize the instantaneous value of a
random variable, consider the following (admittedly con-
trived) example. Let X be a random variable such that

$$\begin{cases} \text{Prob}\{X=N^2\} = 1/N \\ \text{Prob}\{X=0\} = (N-1)/N. \end{cases}$$

Then

$$E(X) = N^2 \cdot (1/N) + 0 \cdot (N-1)/N = N.$$

Thus, as $N \to \infty$, the expected value of X grows without bound, yet the probability that $X = 0$ approaches unity.

It is the characteristic of multiplicative processes such as the one under study that they may behave in exactly the anomalous fashion illustrated by the above example. That is, although $E(N_t)$ may grow without bound as $t \to \infty$, the population may be virtually certain to go to extinction. (Note that this is nothing new for us; we encountered a similar situation while studying the probability of extinction for the "Birth and Death Process".)

To get a better solution to the problem at hand, let us ask a new question. Specifically, we will set out to determine the probability that N_t lies between two values, say K_1 and K_2. Since the log of a variable is a monotonic function

$$\text{Prob}\{K_1 \le N_t \le K_2\} = \text{Prob}\{\ln K_1 \le \ln N_t \le \ln K_2\}.$$

But it follows from the solution for the population size at time t that

$$\ln N_t = \ln N_0 + \sum_{j=1}^{t} \ln R_j$$

so

$$\text{Prob}\{K_1 \le N_t \le K_2\} = \text{Prob}\{\tfrac{1}{t}\ln\tfrac{K_1}{N_0} \le (\overline{\ln R})_t \le \tfrac{1}{t}\ln\tfrac{K_2}{N_0}\}$$

where $(\overline{\ln R})_t$ is the arithmetic mean of the logarithms of the R_t over the previous t generations.

Before continuing let us digress briefly on types of means. Imagine that we have a sample of size n drawn from an infinite population of a random variable called Y with mean μ and standard deviation σ. The sample consists of

-49-

realizations Y_i : $i=1, 2,\ldots,n$.

Arithmetic Mean: $\overline{Y} = \dfrac{1}{n} \sum\limits_{i=1}^{n} Y_i$.

Geometric Mean: $GM_Y = \left\{ \prod\limits_{i=1}^{n} Y_i \right\}^{\frac{1}{n}} = \exp\left\{ \dfrac{1}{n} \sum\limits_{i=1}^{n} \ln Y_i \right\}$.

Harmonic Mean: $HM_Y = n \left\{ \sum\limits_{i=1}^{n} \dfrac{1}{Y_i} \right\}^{-1}$.

If all of the Y_i are not the same, then the arithmetic, geometric and harmonic means are not all the same, even though all attempt to approximate the true mean of the population from which the finite sample is drawn. In fact, it turns out that

$$\overline{Y} > GM_Y > HM_Y \;:\; Y_i \text{ not all identical.}$$

Returning again to the problem at hand, recall that we have assumed that the R_t are independent and identically distributed (iid) with finite mean and variance. It therefore follows that the $\ln R_t$ are also iid with mean, say, $\mu_{\ln R}$ and standard deviation $\sigma_{\ln R}$.

According to the Central Limit Theorem (CLT), since $(\overline{\ln R})_t$ is a sample from the above described distribution, it is approximately normally distributed with mean $\mu_{\ln R}$ and standard deviation $\sigma_{\ln R}/\sqrt{t}$.

Thus, define:

$$\tau = \dfrac{\dfrac{1}{t}\ln\dfrac{N_t}{N_0} - \mu_{\ln R}}{\dfrac{\sigma_{\ln R}}{\sqrt{t}}}$$

and

$$\tau_j = \dfrac{\dfrac{1}{t}\ln\dfrac{K_j}{N_0} - \mu_{\ln R}}{\dfrac{\sigma_{\ln R}}{\sqrt{t}}} \;:\; j=1,2$$

then

$$\text{Prob}\{K_1 \leq N_t \leq K_2\} \approx \text{Prob}\{\tau_1 \leq \tau \leq \tau_2\}.$$

The final expression is just the standardized normal integral between τ_1 and τ_2 which can be looked up in tables of the normal distribution.

Example: A population is growing in an environment which fluctuates between two states at random. The states of the environment are described by $R = 0.5$ and $R = 1.7$, and are assumed to occur with equal likelihood. It therefore follows that

$$\rho = (0.5) \cdot 1/2 + (1.7) \cdot 1/2 = 1.1.$$

And so, after 100 generations

$$E(N_{100}) = \rho^{100} N_0 = 13781 N_0.$$

The actual behavior of the population is quite different.

$$\mu_{\ell n\ R} = (\ell n\ 0.5) \cdot 1/2 + (\ell n\ 1.7) \cdot 1/2 = -0.08126$$

$$\sigma_{\ell n\ R} = \sqrt{(\ell n\ 0.5)^2 \cdot 1/2 + (\ell n\ 1.7)^2 \cdot 1/2 - (-0.08126)^2}$$

$$= 0.6119.$$

Let us calculate the probability that the population after 100 generations is larger than N_0. Thus, let $K_1 = N_0$ and $K_2 = \infty$, which leads to $\tau_1 = 1.33$ and $\tau_2 = \infty$.

Thus, from tables: $\text{Prob}\{N_{100} > N_0\} = 0.092.$

It is possible to interpret our approximate result quite generally. If, as in the example above, we let $K_1 = N_0$ and $K_2 = \infty$, then $\tau_2 = \infty$ and:

$$\begin{cases} \tau_1 \to \infty \text{ as } t \to \infty \text{ if } \mu_{\ell n\ R} < 0, \text{ thus} \\ \quad \text{Prob\{extinction\}} \to 1 \\ \tau_1 \to -\infty \text{ as } t \to \infty \text{ if } \mu_{\ell n\ R} > 0, \text{ thus} \\ \quad \text{Prob\{extinction\}} \to 0. \end{cases}$$

In other words, the probability that the population becomes eventually extinct or grows without bound depends upon whether the true mean of the logarithm of the random variable R is negative or positive. On the other hand, the expected population size eventually becomes extinct or grows without bound according to whether the true mean of the random variable R itself, is less than or greater than unity.

Referring to the definitions of the arithmetic and geometric means, it is clear that

$$E(\ell n\ R) = \ell n\ GM_R = \mu_{\ell n\ R}, \quad \ell n\ E(R) = \ell n\ \overline{R} = \ell n\ \rho.$$

But since $\overline{R} = \rho > \exp\{\mu_{\ell n\ R}\} = GM_R$, it is quite possible to have $\overline{R} > 1$ yet $GM_R < 1$.

A typical case in which this might happen is for population growth in an environment which is ordinarily favorable for growth, but which has an occasional bad year. For example, suppose that nine years out of ten, on average, $R = 1.1$, but in the tenth year, $R = 0.3$. It then follows that $\overline{R} = 1.02$ (so the population expectation tends to grow by 2% per year) but $GM_R = 0.966$ (so the population is sure to go extinct, and fairly rapidly).

We might well wonder what happens if the R_t, instead of being independent, are serially autocorrelated in time. Consider the interesting case of a perfectly cyclic environment with a fixed length cycle of any length. The argument involving the CLT then becomes invalid. However, for such an environment, the rule about the geometric mean determining the eventual population size becomes not a probabilistic statement, but rather exact.

-52-

Imagine that the length of one cycle is k years (time periods), divided between j years with the environment in one state, and k-j years with it in the other state. It then follows immediately from the deterministic solution that

$$N_k = R_a^{\ j} R_b^{\ k-j} N_0 = (GM_R)^k N_0$$

since

$$GM_R = \left\{ \prod_{i=1}^{k} R_i \right\}^{\frac{1}{k}} = \left[R_a^{\ j} R_b^{\ k-j} \right]^{\frac{1}{k}} .$$

For the intervening cases, in which the serial autocorrelation is not perfect, if the environmental cycle length is short compared to t, the time over which the population is observed, then the CLT approximation will be quite good.

The above model always leads to either extinction or unbounded growth, since the model excludes any density dependence. We would next like to include such density dependence. Unfortunately, this will create substantial mathematical problems. We will therefore be forced to settle for some informative, but not entirely satisfactory calculations.

We will study the Logistic Differential Equation, and will include the idea of environment variability by letting the Carrying Capacity of the environment be a function of time; thus

$$\frac{dN(t)}{dt} = r_0 N(t) \left[1 - N(t)/K(t) \right].$$

Before attempting an analytic solution, let us use what we know about the solution of the L.D.E. with a constant Carrying Capacity to try to anticipate the results. For mathematical reasons, we will be forced in the analytic investigation to study not random but rather perfectly periodic (sinusoidal) fluctuations in $K(t)$. We therefore will look initially at a population which lives in a place where the environment shifts back and forth between two

states in a regular manner. Imagine that it takes a time T
to go through one full cycle, with half the time spent in
one state, then the other half in the other state.

Recall that the graphical picture of the solution to
the L.D.E. looks as shown below, for a variety of initial
population sizes.

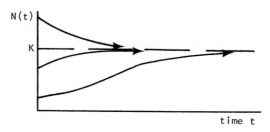

Recall also that the amount of time taken to approach the
Carrying Capacity depends upon the value of the parameter
r_0; the larger r_0, the faster the asymptote is approached.

We will consider two limiting cases:

    1. $r_0 T \gg 1$: This corresponds to the case where
the population has the potential
to grow very rapidly, and where
the environment spends a long time
in each of its two states.

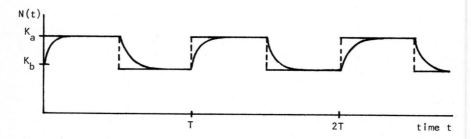

Notice that the population spends most of its time
very near to the present value of the Carrying Capacity;
that is, it tends to 'track' the environmental fluctuations.

2. $r_0 T \ll 1$: This corresponds to the case where the population can only grow very slowly, and where the state of the environment switches frequently.

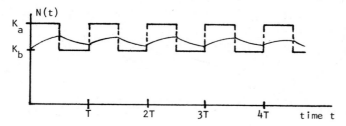

Notice that the population never has a change to get near to the Carrying Capacity, as before very much growth has occurred, the environment has again switched states; thus this time the population 'averages' the environmental fluctuations.

Analytic treatment: Although the L.D.E. is nonlinear, it can be made linear by the substitution $y(t) = 1/N(t) \rightarrow$

$$\frac{dy}{dt} + r_0 y = r_0/K(t) : N(0) = N_0 \rightarrow y(0) = 1/N_0.$$

Integrating the D.E. by means of Integrating Factor and using the initial condition leads to

$$y(t) = \frac{1}{N_0} \exp\{-r_0 t\} + r_0 \int_0^t \frac{\exp\{-r_0(t-\tau)\}\, d\tau}{K(\tau)}.$$

Notice that as $t \rightarrow \infty$, the first term on the R.H.S. drops out (goes to zero). This simply means that after a long time has passed, the effect of the initial population size becomes unimportant. Since we are more interested in the effects of the fluctuating environment than the initial conditions, we look only at the long time solution:

$$y(t) \sim r_0 \int_0^t \frac{\exp\{-r_0(t-\tau)\}\, d\tau}{K(\tau)} : N(t) = 1/y(t)$$

along with $\quad K(\tau) = K_0 + K_1 \cos\{2\pi\tau/T\} : K_0 > K_1$.

We proceed now to consider the same two limiting cases that we looked at with the approximate graphical method.

    1. $r_0 T \gg 1$: slow oscillations/rapid growth.

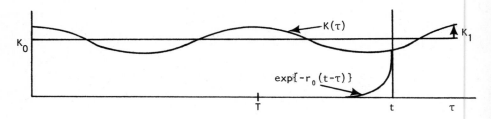

Since $\displaystyle\lim_{t\to\infty} r_0 \int_0^t \exp\{-r_0(t-\tau)\}\ d\tau \to 1$,

replace the exponential by a Dirac Delta function, $\delta(t-\tau)$; thus

$$y(t) \sim \int_0^{t+} \frac{\delta(t-\tau)\ d\tau}{K_0 + K_1 \cos\{2\pi\tau/T\}}$$

leads to

$$N(t) \sim K_0 + K_1 \cos\{2\pi t/T\}.$$

Thus, the long time behavior when $r_0 T \gg 1$ has the population exactly 'tracking' the environment.

    2. $r_0 T \ll 1$: rapid oscillations/slow growth.

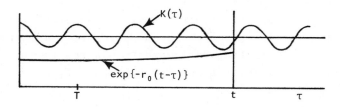

Since the exponential is nearly constant over any one cycle of $K(\tau)$, the average value of $y(t)$ will about equal average over one cycle; thus

$$\langle y(t) \rangle \sim \frac{1}{T} \int_0^T \frac{d\tau}{K_0 + K_1 \cos\{2\pi\tau/T\}}$$

which leads to

$$\langle N(t) \rangle \sim \sqrt{K_0^2 - K_1^2} \;.$$

Thus, the long time behavior when $r_0 T \ll 1$ shows that the population tends to 'average' the environmental fluctuations.

The one interesting new fact that we learned from the analytic treatment which was not accessible to the graphical method is that for the second case, the 'averaging' puts the mean population size not at K_0 as we might expect, but always below it, by an amount which depends upon K_1.

Problems

1. Show that for a random variable Y with mean μ and variance σ^2

   $E(\ln Y) < \ln E(Y).$

2. A population grows according to the relation: $N_t = R_t N_{t-1}$. Assume that the environment fluctuates randomly between two states, one with R = 1.1, the other with R = 0.3. If the population is subject to the former type of environment nine years out of ten, find the expected population size after 100 seasons, and the probability that the population is larger than it was when it started, also after 100 seasons.

3.   Starting with the Logistic D.E.:

$$\frac{dN}{dt} = r_0 N(1 - N/K)$$

make the substitution $N = 1/y$ to convert the equation
to a linear form. Then solve for $N(t)$, assuming that
r_0 and K are constants. Compare your answer to the
one found earlier.

References

The models discussed in this section are drawn from
three sources. These are:

Levins, R., "The Effect of Random Variations of Different
    Types on Population Growth", Proceedings of the
    National Academy of Sciences, Volume 62, pp. 1061-1065,
    1969.

    The mathematics in this paper is among the most
    sophisticated in any of the references. It should
    probably be approached with care.

Lewontin, R.C. and D. Cohen, "On Population Growth in a
    Randomly Varying Environment", Proceedings of the
    National Academy of Sciences, Volume 62, pp. 1056-1060,
    1969.

    The material in this paper forms the first portion of
    the text in this section of this monograph.

May, R.M., "Models for Single Species", Chapter 2 of
    Theoretical Ecology, Principles and Applications, R.M.
    May (ed), Saunders Co., Philadelphia, PA, 1976.

    In section 2.5, the models discussed in the latter
    portion of this section of this monograph are outlined,
    though the mathematical details are omitted.

6 Stable Points, Stable Cycles and Chaos

We proceed now to look at the dynamics of a population with a life history in which successive generations do not overlap one another. Some types of fishes, such as the salmon, as well as many kinds of insects live in this way. The parent generation leaves its eggs before it dies in the fall. The eggs then winter over, and the young emerge in the spring. The potential for bizarre population trajectories exists; consider for example the thirteen year periodic cicada. Our goal will be to try to discover the range of behavior which is possible.

It will be possible to proceed without writing down a very detailed specification of our mathematical model. Quite generally, we will look at models of the form

$$N(t+1) = f[N(t)]$$

where all that is really required is that $f(\cdot)$ be a function which starts off at zero, rises to a single maximum and then falls off again. It will also be convenient to think of the function $f(\cdot)$ containing a "tuning parameter". The Logistic $\Delta.E.$ it will be recalled contains a function of the appropriate form, and the "tuning parameter" is represented by r_0. A great many other realistic models for single species population growth with discrete generations are also of the proper form.

In order that $f(\cdot)$ be of the form we demand it must be non-linear. Thus as usual, we proceed by first doing a linearized stability analysis. In our present notation, this is done as follows:

Equilibrium: Set $N(t + 1) = N(t) = N^{(1)}$,

so that
$$N^{(1)} = f[N^{(1)}].$$

This is an equation (algebraic or transcendental) which is solved to locate the equilibrium point.

N.B. For the L.Δ.E., this yields the result $N^{(1)} = K$.

Stability: Set $N(t) = N^{(1)} + x(t)$,

so that
$$N^{(1)} + x(t+1) = f[N^{(1)} + x(t)]$$
$$= N^{(1)} + \{(df/dN)|_{N=N^{(1)}}\}x(t)$$
$$+ \cdots$$

Linearize
$$x(t+1) = \{(df/dN)|_{N=N^{(1)}}\} x(t)$$

Stable if $|(df/dN)_{N=N^{(1)}}| < 1$.

N.B. For the L.Δ.E., this yields the result $|1 - r_0| < 1$ for stability.

We are now at the end of what we know how to do with linearized stability analysis. So long as the value of the "tuning parameter" is small enough, the stability condition will be satisfied, and the point $N = N^{(1)}$ will be a stable point. Once the "tuning parameter" becomes too big, the solution becomes unstable, <u>and</u> the linearized solution breaks down.

However, for a function $f(\cdot)$ of the form prescribed, we can in fact continue. To do so, we examine the equation

$$N(t+2) = f[N(t+1)] = f[f[N(t)]]$$
$$= f^{(2)}[N(t)].$$

Once again, perform a linearized stability analysis.

Equilibrium: Set $N(t+2) = N(t) = N^{(2)}$,

so that

$$N^{(2)} = f^{(2)}[N^{(2)}].$$

This is an equation which is solved to locate the equilibrium points. One solution will be $N^{(2)} = N^{(1)}$. In addition, there will be two other roots which will be extraneous (i.e. complex) in the regime where $N^{(1)}$ was stable, and real where $N^{(1)}$ was unstable.

N.B.   For the L.Δ.E., when $r_0 > 2$, there are three equilibrium points instead of just one.

Stability: Set $N(t) = N_i^{(2)} + x_i(t)$: $i = 1, 2, 3$.

Follow through linearized stability analysis as before:

$$x_i(t+2) = \{(df^{(2)}/dN)|_{N = N_i^{(2)}}\} \, x_i(t).$$

Stable if $\left| (df^{(2)}/dN)|_{N = N_i^{(2)}} \right| < 1$.

It will always turn out that the single root $N^{(2)} = N^{(1)}$ will become unstable just as the other two roots appear (i.e. become real valued). These two roots will be stable, up to a critical value of the "tuning parameter" at which point they too become unstable.

N.B. For the L.Δ.E., the region of stability for the roots $N_i^{(2)}$ extends over $2 < r_0 < 2.449$.

What have we just discovered? Perhaps the best way to visualize the finding is to think about turning the "tuning parameter" up. At first, there is a single stable point called $N^{(1)}$. At a certain value of the "tuning parameter" this point ceases to be stable, but is replaced by a pair of points, $N_1^{(2)}$ and $N_2^{(2)}$ (which will be one on either side of $N^{(1)}$). At first, these two points are stable, but only in a _very_ special way. Specifically, the population will alternate between them, and if disturbed a tiny bit, will return to the "period two" mode.

Perhaps the best way to visualize what is going on is to resort to a graphical solution. The method is formally identical to the one employed while discussing the two age-group model, except that the labels on the axes have been changed. Otherwise, the interpretation is identical.

The illustration below shows a plot of $f[N]$ along with the line $N(t) = N(t+1)$. Their point of intersection represents the equilibrium point denoted $N^{(1)}$. As before, linearized stability analysis amounts to replacing the function $f[N]$ by a straight line which is tangent at the intersection point. Solutions for either the non-linear or the linear approximation are found by successively projecting first vertically, then horizontally.

N.B. Vertical projection until $f[N]$ (or its approximation) is reached amounts to finding the next value of the population size, given the present value. Horizontal projection to the 45 degree line then increments the index (time) by one unit.

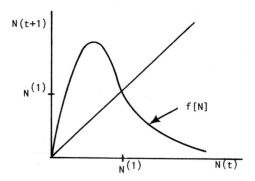

We must next attempt to see what happens as the "tuning parameter" is increased, until it passes through its first critical point when $N^{(1)}$ becomes unstable (bifurcation occurs) and the solution passes to the doubly periodic case. To see this, we wish to look directly at the function $f^{(2)}[N]$. The graphical construction of this function is straightforward, though somewhat confusing.

Imagine proceeding as follows. First, on a set of axes draw the function $f[N]$ and the 45 degree line (as above). Then, subdivide the horizontal axis into many small segments by applying a uniform grid. At the first grid point, project up until $f[N]$ is reached. Then project horizontally until the 45 degree line is reached, and then project vertically again until $f[N]$ is reached. Finally, project horizontally until the original vertical line from the first grid point is intersected. This point lies on $f^{(2)}[N]$. Repeat for each of the many grid points, and then fill in the iterated function $f^{(2)}[N]$.

The figure below illustrates typical functions $f^{(2)}[N]$ for values of the "tuning parameter" below critical, at critical (where instability occurs) and within the stable region for the doubly periodic oscillation mode, plotted against N.

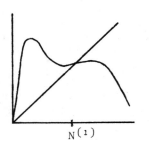 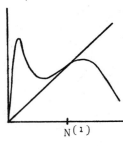 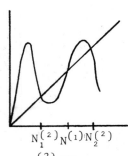

$N^{(1)}$ $\qquad\qquad$ $N^{(1)}$ $\qquad\qquad$ $N_1^{(2)}N^{(1)}N_2^{(2)}$

Note that only in the third figure does $f^{(2)}[N]$ actually cross the 45 degree line more than once. All figures have a crossing at $N^{(1)}$, the third also has ones at $N_1^{(2)}$ and $N_2^{(2)}$.

Stability for the doubly periodic case shown in the third figure is ascertained graphically by looking at the slope of the functional curve as it crosses the 45 degree line. It is not difficult to show that the slope is identical at both new crossings. Once these become more negative than -1, again bifurcation occurs, this time to a period four mode. As the "tuning parameter" is increased, successive bifurcations to period 8, 16, 32, . . . occur. Note that each successive bifurcation requires a smaller increment in the value of the "tuning parameter".

N.B.   For the L.Δ.E. the regimes are as follows:

$\qquad$ $2.449 < r_0 < 2.544$: Period 4 oscillation.

$\qquad$ $2.544 < r_0 < 2.564$: Period 8 oscillation.

$\qquad$ $2.564 < r_0 < 2.570$: Periods 16, 32, 64, ...

Note that in solving analytically for these values, it is never necessary to perform the stability phase of the linearized stability analysis. This is because as one mode of oscillation becomes unstable, it branches to the mode which has double the period. Thus to find the range of the "tuning parameter" for the period 2^n oscillations, find the critical value of the "tuning parameter" for the inception of period 2^n by solving

$$N^{(2^n)} = f^{(2^n)}\left[N^{(2^n)}\right].$$

This gives the lower limit of the "tuning parameter". Then repeat with n replaced by n+1 in the above expression. This gives the upper limit of the "tuning parameter".

Comments:

1. The reason that when the period k mode of oscillation becomes unstable, it gives way to an initially stable period 2k mode can be seen from the fact that

$$(df^{(2k)}/dN)\big|_{N=N_i^{(k)}}$$

$$= \left[(df^{(k)}/dN)\big|_{N=N_i^{(k)}}\right]^2 \; : \; i=1,\; 2,\ldots,k.$$

This says that the slope of $f^{(2k)}$ at the fixed points of $f^{(k)}$ is just the square of the slope of $f^{(k)}$ at its own fixed points. Further, it is not hard to show by using the chain rule, that these slopes are all the same for all i. (Call the slopes $\lambda(k)$ and $\lambda(2k)$, respectively.) Consider the period k mode. If it is stable, then $-1 < \lambda(k) < +1$, thus $0 < \lambda(2k) < +1$, so the 'kink' in $f^{(2k)}$ does not yet intersect the 45 degree line. Once the period k mode becomes unstable, $\lambda(k) < -1$, and so $\lambda(2k) > +1$, so the 'kink' in $f^{(2k)}$ now intersects the 45 degree line at two points, exhibiting the bifurcation of the period k mode to the period 2k mode.

2. Although the plots of the m-times-composed function $f^{(m)}$ are useful for visualizing the location and progression of the fixed points,

they tend to hide the time histories of populations experiencing period m mode oscillations. What we would discover if we drew the
basic function f[N] with the "tuning parameter" at a level which leads to stable period m oscillations, and then located the m
fixed points of $f^{(m)}$ is that the population
size in successive generations cycles through
the m fixed points in a serial order. Examples of time traces for period 1, 2 and 4
modes are shown below.

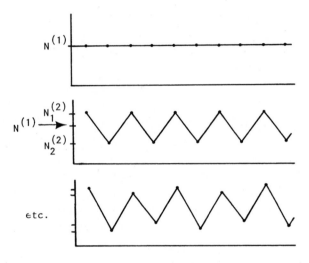

3. It is important to realize the distinction
    between the period 2 mode and the neutrally
    stable, oscillatory behavior which is often
    predicted by a linearized stability analysis.
    Note that the neutrally stable result only
    occurs for the mathematically pathological
    case of a precise value of the "tuning para-
    meter", while the period 2 mode is persistent
    over a range of values of the "tuning para-

meter." In addition, the amplitude of the neutrally stable oscillation is determined entirely by the size of the initial disturbance from equilibrium, while the period 2 mode has its amplitude determined by the parameters of the model. These distinctions will be extremely important when we discuss multi-species models. We will subsequently discard neutrally stable oscillations as mathematical pathologies, while the analog of the period 2 (and higher) modes will be called nonlinear limit cycles.

What happens as we keep on increasing the value of the "tuning parameter"?

As we noted earlier, the regime of the "tuning parameter" which leads to period 1, 2, 4, 8, ... modes of oscillation become smaller and smaller. Eventually, we reach a value of the "tuning parameter" for which we predict an infinite number of fixed points, some of which are stable, others unstable. The result is that there are an uncountable number of points which lead to aperiodic behavior.

Thus, no matter how long the population evolves, its time history never repeats itself. The particular trace which results depends upon the initial population size. Two populations which differ from one another by a vanishingly small amount initially, after a long time, can have radically different traces. In fact, the traces which result are (almost) indistinguishable from the sample function of a stochastic process! Such behavior has been aptly called chaos.

It is not difficult to determine if a particular function can support chaotic behavior. All that is necessary is that the function lead to stable, period 3 mode oscillations. In the figure below, we show such a situation.

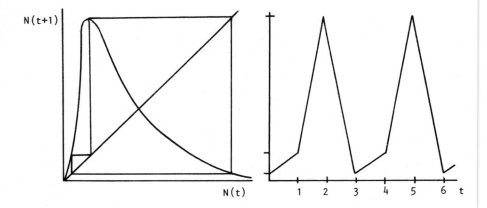

In a truly remarkable theorem, which we will discuss shortly, it is shown that the existence of period 3 mode oscillations ensures that there also exist all other period modes.

Finding the critical value of the "tuning parameter" which leads to chaotic behavior is straightforward, and not particularly interesting. We therefore omit a careful discussion, and mention only that a good approximate formula has been found. If we call the critical value of the "tuning parameter", r_c, then the regime of chaos starts when

$$\lambda^{(k)}[r_c] \simeq -1.5$$

where $\lambda^{(k)}[r]$ is the slope of $f^{(k)}[N]$ at any of its period k fixed points, when the "tuning parameter" is equal to r. The approximation improves as k increases.

N.B. For the L.Δ.E., $\lambda^{(1)}[r_c] = 1 - r_c = -1.5$ leads to $r_c = 2.5$. The asymptotic result is $r_c = 2.570$. Thus even with k = 1 the approximation is rather good.

Before looking at the theorem which says, period 3 leads to chaos, we make a few observations concerning the physical implications of our findings.

1. All of the interesting results which we found,
    such as multiple periodicity and chaos, dis-
    appear if we treat time as a continuous vari-
    able, or consider only the linearized equa-
    tions.

2. The potential of a purely deterministic model
    to yield almost stochastic-like behavior sug-
    gests that when considering the actual census
    data for a population which lives in discrete
    time, it will be impossible to sort the
    actual random part from the peculiar dynamics.

We now embark on a rather lengthy digression in which
we consider the question: given a continuous function f
which has fixed points of period k, must it also have fixed
points of period $j \neq k$?

One result follows easily. Assume that f has a periodic point p of period k, so there is a sequence of iterates:

$$p, \ f(p), \ f^{(2)}(p), \ . \ . \ ., \ f^{(k-1)}(p), \ f^{(k)}(p) = p.$$

Next, suppose that $f(p)>p$. Then there must be a point
$q = f^{(i)}(p)$ in the sequence such that $f(q) = f^{(i+1)}(p) <
f^{(i)}(p) = q$ or else the sequence would continue to increase
and could not return to p. But then, since f is a continuous function, by the Intermediate Value Theorem (IVT)
there is a point r between p and q where $f(r) = r$. (A symmetric argument clearly disposes of the case where $f(p)<p$.)
Thus we have

Period k leads to Period 1, for all k.

The theorem which we would like to demonstrate is very
simply stated as

Period 3 leads to Period k, for all k.

In order to proceed toward a proof of this theorem, consider the continuous function f which has a fixed point of period k. A typical example for a period 5 case is shown below.

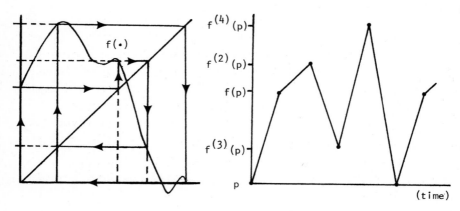

In general, imagine starting with p and then spreading the iterates of p along the real line. Without loss of generality we will assume that p is the smallest such iterate. The iterates divide the line into k-1 intervals, which we call, from left to right, I_1, I_2, ..., I_{k-1}. Thus for the information in the figure above, this would become

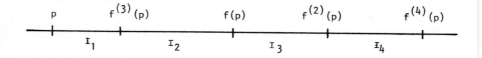

Next, consider $f(I_1)$. For our example, I_1 has endpoints p and $f^{(3)}(p)$, which get mapped respectively into $f(p)$ and $f^{(4)}(p)$. Hence by the IVT, $f(I_1)$ must include all points between $f(p)$ and $f^{(4)}(p)$, thus

$$f(I_1) \supset I_3 \cup I_4$$

similarly $\quad f(I_2) \supset I_4$

$$f(I_3) \supset I_2 \cup I_3$$
$$f(I_4) \supset I_1.$$

An extremely useful way to convey this information is by means of a digraph (directed graph), with vertices corresponding to the intervals, and edges from I_i to I_j if $f(I_i) \supset I_j$. Thus for our example

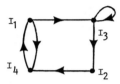

Notice that the process which we have employed, starting from the function and ending with the digraph, is completely general. It works for any continuous function and any periodicity k.

We will not bother to prove the fact that if the digraph has a non-repetitive cycle of length j, then the function f must have periodic points of period j. Note that cycles are allowed to pass through a vertex or along an edge more than once. "Non-repetitive" means that we do not allow cycles obtained by tracing a cycle of smaller length over and over. This is illustrated below, for cycles of length 8 on the graph developed above.

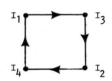

Twice around - illegal

$I_1 I_3 I_2 I_4 I_1 I_3 I_2 I_4 I_1$

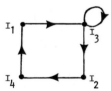

4 times around small loop - legal

$I_1 I_3 I_3 I_3 I_3 I_3 I_2 I_4 I_1$

It is now extremely easy to prove our theorem that

Period 3 leads to Period k, for all k.

For period 3, only two distinct orderings are possible for the sequence p, f(p), $f^{(2)}(p)=p$ (Recall that without loss of generality we may assume that p is the smallest of the three.)   There are thus just 2!=2 orderings, as shown below.

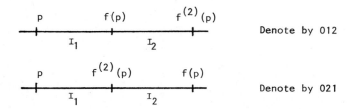

But these are really not distinct, as illustrated below:

$$012 \xrightarrow{\text{flip the line}} 210 \xrightarrow{\text{change names}} 021.$$

Referring to the case denoted by 012 above, it should be clear that

$$f(I_1) \supset I_2$$
$$f(I_2) \supset I_1 \cup I_2.$$

The associated digraph is thus

which is easily seen to have cycles of <u>all</u> lengths, which proves the theorem.

What about period 5? It is not hard to deduce that there are 12 distinct digraphs, ten of which contain the period 3 digraph as a subgraph, and thus have fixed points of all periodicities. The other two digraphs are shown below. Note that the one on the left has non-repetitive cycles of all lengths, and thus implies fixed points of all orders. The one on the right, however, does <u>not</u> permit cycles of length 3, thus

Period 5 leads to all periods except 3.

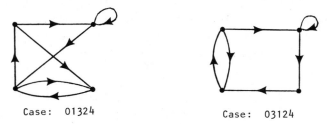

Case: 01324   Case: 03124

Several other theorems are easily proven:

1. Every "periodic point" digraph has a 1-cycle (loop).
2. Every "periodic point" digraph has a 2-cycle.
3. Period k leads to period 2 for all k>2.
4. No even period need imply any odd period > 1.
5. No odd period need imply any <u>lower</u> odd period > 1.

Examples for numbers 4 and 5 are illustrated below:

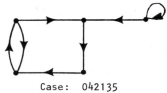

Case: 042135
all even periods, but no odd periods > 1.

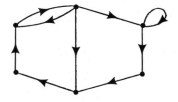

Case: 0531246

Period 7, but not periods 3, 5.

Problems

1. Start with the Logistic Δ.E.:

$$N_{t+1} = N_t \left[1 + r_0 (1 - N_t/K) \right]$$

   a. Perform a linearized stability analysis. From this determine the location of the fixed point (equilibrium), the range of the parameter r_0 which leads to this fixed point, and the stability properties of the fixed point.

   b. Determine the equation which describes the period 2 mode (the doubly periodic case).

   c. Using the equation found in part b, find the critical value of r_0 at which bifurcation into the period 2 takes place, and find the location of the period 2 fixed points as a function of r_0.

2. Using the Logistic Δ.E. (above), make an estimate of the value $r = r_c$ where the chaotic regime starts, using the formula

$$\lambda^{(2)} \left[r_c \right] = -1.5$$

   where $\lambda^{(2)} \left[r \right]$ is the slope of $f^{(2)}$ evaluated at any of the period 2 critical points, as a function of r. To make the estimate, evaluate the slope at $r = 2.5$ and $r = 2.6$ and then interpolate.

3. Draw the periodic point digraph for the following:

   a. period 5 fixed point denoted by 01423.
   b. period 5 fixed point denoted by 01243.
   c. period 9 fixed point denoted by 075312468.

   In each case, note what periods are not possible.

References

The rather remarkable behavior discussed in this section has interested mathematicians for many years. New interest was stimulated recently by the publication of the first paper listed below.

Li, T.Y. and J.A. Yorke, "Period Three Implies Chaos", American Mathematical Monthly, Volume 82, pp. 985-992, 1975.

In this paper the proof discussed in the latter portion of this section of this monograph is proved in rather abstract terms.

May, R.M., "Biological Populations with Nonoverlapping Generations: Stable Points, Stable Cycles and Chaos", Science, Volume 186, pp. 645-647, November 15, 1974.

The attention of the biological community was drawn to the unusual dynamics of certain difference equations by the publication of this short paper.

May, R.M., "Simple Mathematical Models with Very Complicated Dynamics", Nature, Volume 261, pp. 459-467, June 10, 1976.

This paper extends the material discussed in the paper noted above by the same author. In addition, a useful review of the literature is provided.

Straffin, P.D., Jr., "Periodic Points of Continuous Functions", Mathematics Magazine, Volume 51, pp 99-105, March, 1978.

In this paper, the procedure employing directed graphs which is described in this section of this monograph is developed in detail.

7 Introduction to Two-Species Models: Predator-Prey

No species of animal lives in complete isolation. Since all animals must eat to live, all must interact, if not with other animals, then with plants. The model which we will build and then study considers the situation where one animal population serves as food for another. We will stylize the discussion by thinking of the predators as foxes, and the prey as rabbits. Note that the predators could equally well be rabbits and the "prey" lettuce. The important point is that the one species serves as the food for the other, and both grow according to some reasonable set of biological laws. The model is somewhat unrealistic in that few ecological systems are so simple as to have just two species present.

Recall from the single species population models discussed earlier that the exact description of the growth process is represented by the ordinary differential equation

$$\frac{dN}{dt} = r(N,t)N$$

where N is the population size at time t, and r is the

Intrinsic Rate of Population Growth.

To extend this to the case of two interacting species, say rabbits and foxes, is straightforward. Simply let

R(t) = number of rabbits in population at time t.

F(t) = number of foxes in population at time t.

Further, assume as we have done all along that the Intrinsic Rate of Population Growth for each species is independent of explicit time dependence, and varies only with population size. Thus, quite generally we say

$r_R(R,F)$ = Intrinsic Rate for the rabbits.

$r_F(R,F)$ = Intrinsic Rate for the foxes.

It then follows from our definitions and the single species model that the basic form for the governing equations is:

$$\frac{dR}{dt} = r_R(R,F)R$$

$$\frac{dF}{dt} = r_F(R,F)F.$$

We must next consider the form for the respective Intrinsic Rates. We will incorporate the following simple assumptions into these relations:

1. In the absence of foxes, the rabbit population tends to grow without restriction.
2. The effect of the presence of foxes on the rabbit population is to reduce the rate of growth in proportion to the number of foxes present.
3. In the absence of rabbits, the fox population tends to die off due to starvation.
4. The effect of the presence of rabbits on the fox population is to increase the rate of growth in proportion to the number of rabbits present.

The first pair of assumptions suggest that we choose to model the Intrinsic Rate of Growth for the rabbits by the expression:

$$r_R(R,F) = a - \alpha F : a \text{ and } \alpha \text{ positive constants.}$$

Similarly, the second pair of assumptions suggest

$$r_F(R,F) = -b + \beta R : b \text{ and } \beta \text{ positive constants.}$$

The equations which must be solved result when these expressions are substituted into the governing equations

$$\frac{dR}{dt} = (a - \alpha F)R$$

$$: a, b, \alpha, \beta > 0.$$

$$\frac{dF}{dt} = (-b + \beta R)F$$

Identify these as a pair of coupled, non-linear, ordinary differential equations. Although we will figure out a way to solve these completely, let us assume for the moment that we do not know how to do so, and see what we can learn from a Stability Analysis.

Stability Analysis: We first seek the equilibrium point(s). These occur at those values of R and F which cause dR/dt = 0 and dF/dt = 0 simultaneously. Thus, set the above equations equal to zero to get:

$$(a - \alpha F)R = 0$$
$$(-b + \beta R)F = 0.$$

Even though these are non-linear algebraic equations, their simple form permits a solution by observation. Clearly, they are simultaneously satisfied by two sets of values: (R = 0 and F = 0) or (R = b/β and F = a/α). These two points are the equilibrium points. Obviously the one with both species absent is of less interest than the one with both species present.

We therefore investigate the stability of the equilibrium at R = b/β and F = a/α. To do so we first define a new pair of variables with origins at the equilibrium point. Let

$$R(t) = \frac{b}{\beta} + \rho(t)$$

$$F(t) = \frac{a}{\alpha} + \phi(t).$$

Substitute these definitions into the governing equations to get the new set of equations written in terms of the variables ρ and ϕ

$$\frac{d\rho}{dt} = -\alpha\phi\left(\frac{b}{\beta} + \rho\right)$$

$$\frac{d\phi}{dt} = \beta\rho\left(\frac{a}{\alpha} + \phi\right).$$

Next we assume that $|\rho| \ll b/\beta$ and $|\phi| \ll a/\alpha$ and linearize to get

$$\frac{d\rho}{dt} = \frac{-\alpha b}{\beta}\phi$$

$$\frac{d\phi}{dt} = \frac{a\beta}{\alpha}\rho.$$

The nature of the stability of the equilibrium at $R = b/\beta$, $F = a/\alpha$ is found by solving this pair of coupled D.E.s. Numerous methods are available; we will illustrate several.

One way to proceed is to reduce the pair of equations to a single, second order equation. This is accomplished, for example, by differentiating the first equation with respect to t, and then using the second equation to eliminate $d\phi/dt$. This leads to

$$\frac{d^2\rho}{dt^2} + (ab)\rho = 0.$$

This equation occurs so often that it should be recognized, and its solution written down directly. We proceed by listing this solution without derivation (though it is a simple exercise to verify that is satisfies the D.E.)

$$\rho(t) = C_1 \sin\sqrt{ab}\, t + C_2 \cos\sqrt{ab}\, t$$

where C_1 and C_2 are constants which are determined by the initial disturbance away from equilibrium. For example, let us assume that at time $t = 0$ the rabbit population exceeds its equilibrium value by a small amount ρ_0 and the fox population is in equilibrium. Thus $\rho(0) = \rho_0$, and $\phi(0) = 0$. This tells us immediately that $C_2 = \rho_0$.

We next use the first of the linearized equations to find $\phi(t)$. By differentiating our solution for $\rho(t)$ we see that

$$\phi(t) = -\frac{\beta}{\alpha} \sqrt{a/b} \{C_1 \cos\sqrt{ab}\, t - \rho_0 \sin\sqrt{ab}\, t \}.$$

But at $t = 0$ $\phi(0) = 0$, thus $C_1 = 0$. Thus we have found that

$$\rho(t) = \rho_0 \cos\sqrt{ab}\, t$$

$$\phi(t) = \phi_0 \sin\sqrt{ab}\, t$$

where we have defined $\phi_0 = \rho_0 \beta\sqrt{a/b}/\alpha$. Before looking at other ways to solve the linearized D.E.s, let us make a few observations:

1. The linearized solution for ρ and ϕ neither grows nor shrinks, but rather just continues to oscillate. This implies that the equilibrium is neutrally stable.

2. The period of the oscillations T is then given by $\sqrt{ab}\ T = 2\pi$ which yields

$$T = \frac{2\pi}{\sqrt{ab}}.$$

3. The oscillations of the rabbit and fox populations are 90° out of phase, with the rabbits leading the foxes.

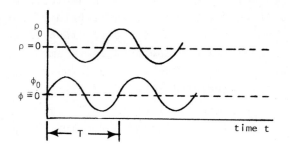

4. We can exhibit the results another way. Elim-
    inate explicit time dependence by forming the
    expression

    $$(\rho/\rho_0)^2 + (\phi/\phi_0)^2$$
    $$= \cos^2\sqrt{ab}\, t + \sin^2\sqrt{ab}\, t = 1.$$

    Recognize that this is the equation for an
    ellipse in (ρ, ϕ) co-ordinates. The plot,
    which we shall refer to as the "trajectory"
    in population space looks like:

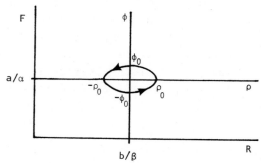

5. It is also possible to determine the direc-
    tion of motion in population space. Recall
    the first linearized D.E.,

    $$\frac{d\rho}{dt} = -\frac{\alpha b}{\beta}\, \phi.$$

Thus, at the point on the trajectory $(0, \phi_0)$, $d\rho/dt < 0$ since α, β and b are all positive constants. Therefore, the trajectory is traversed counter-clockwise in population space, as shown above.

6. Note that the time it takes to traverse one cycle (the period) is independent of the values of ρ_0 and ϕ_0.

We next illustrate a general procedure for solving linear, ordinary differential equations with constant coefficients, such as the one

$$\frac{d^2\rho}{dt^2} + (ab)\ \rho = 0.$$

Assume that the solution can be written in the form $\rho = A \exp\{\lambda t\}$ where A and λ are constants to be determined. Substituting the assumed form of the solution into the D.E. provides an algebraic equation called the Characteristic Equation

$$\lambda^2 + ab = 0.$$

The roots of this equation are the values of λ sought, and here are

$$\lambda_1 = i\sqrt{ab}, \ \lambda_2 = -i\sqrt{ab} : i = \sqrt{-1}.$$

Therefore the solution is given by:

$$\rho(t) = A_1 \exp\{i\sqrt{ab}\ t\} + A_2 \exp\{-i\sqrt{ab}\ t\}$$

where A_1 and A_2 are (possibly complex) constants determined by the initial conditions, but which for physical reasons must yield a real solution. Note that at first sight this solution appears to be different than the one found earlier. In fact, it is precisely the same.

In order that the solution be purely real, it is not hard to see that A_1 and A_2 must be complex conjugates. For example, let

$$A_1 = \tfrac{1}{2}(C_2 - iC_1), \ A_2 = \tfrac{1}{2}(C_2 + iC_1)$$

and recall the definition of the complex exponential

$$\exp\{u \pm iv\} = \exp\{u\}(\cos v \pm i \sin v)$$

Following a bit of algebra, it turns out using these definitions that

$$\rho(t) = C_1 \sin\sqrt{ab}\, t + C_2 \cos\sqrt{ab}\, t$$

which is precisely the same as before. Once again, several comments are in order:

1. If instead of being second order the ODE is n^{th} order the procedure is still exactly the same. The only difficulty is that the Characteristic Equation is also n^{th} order, so extracting the roots may be laborious.

2. Often the ODE is presented in the form of a set of n first order equations. In fact this was the case for our problem. There is no reason to convert to an nth order equation. Simply deal with the set of equations as above. The algebraic system which results will be homogeneous, hence the determinant of the coefficient matrix must be zero for a solution to exist. The equation which results when the determinant of the coefficient matrix is set equal to zero is the Characteristic Equation. Let us quickly go through this ex-exercise for the linearized Predator-Prey equations:

    $$\frac{d\rho}{dt} = -\frac{\alpha b}{\beta}\, \phi$$

    $$\frac{d\phi}{dt} = \frac{a\beta}{\alpha}\, \rho.$$

    Let $\rho = A_1 \exp\{\lambda t\}$ and $\phi = A_2 \exp\{\lambda t\}$ to get (in matrix form)

$$\begin{bmatrix} -\lambda & -\alpha b/\beta \\ +a\beta/\alpha & -\lambda \end{bmatrix} \cdot \begin{bmatrix} A_1 \\ A_2 \end{bmatrix} = 0.$$

Clearly, the determinant of the coefficient matrix is

$$\lambda^2 + ab = 0.$$

3. The most important point to appreciate here is that it is not necessary to go through the entire solution process to do a Stability Analysis. In fact, all we need to do is find the roots of the Characteristic Equation. This is because regardless of the precise values of the constants A_1, A_2, . . . the nature of the solution is determined by the behavior of the exponentials which are in turn governed by the values of λ_1, λ_2, . . .
    So to do a Stability Analysis in the future, find the roots of the Characteristic Equation, and then plot these in the complex λ plane. By reference to the definition of the complex exponential it is then apparent that:

    a. If <u>all</u> roots are in the LHP (left half plane) the equilibrium is stable.

    b. If <u>any</u> root is in the RHP the equilibrium is unstable.

    c. If <u>all</u> roots are in the LHP except for some which lie on imaginary axis, equilibrium is neutral.

    d. If <u>all</u> roots are on the real axis, solution does not oscillate.

    e. If <u>any</u> root is off the real axis, solution oscillates. Note that complex roots always appear in conjugate pairs, thus there must be an even number of roots off the real axis.

For our problem, the complex λ plane looks like:

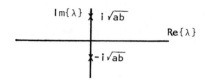

For most population systems we would have to interpret the behavior of the system from the stability analysis alone because a complete solution would not be possible. We would therefore attempt to find the nature of the equilibrium at the other equilibrium point $(0,0)$ and then decide what is implied. Conveniently, the Predator-Prey model permits a complete solution which is useful for purposes of comparison with what is learned by Stability Analysis.

Complete Solution: The critical step is to notice from the original governing equations that explicit time dependence can be eliminated by dividing the first equation by the second to get

$$\frac{dR}{dF} = \frac{(a - \alpha F)R}{(-b + \beta R)F} .$$

Just as with the first simple population models considered, this D.E. can be separated and integrated

$$\int(-b/R + \beta)dR = \int(a/F - \alpha)dF$$

$$a \ln F - \alpha F + b \ln R - \beta R = \ln k$$

$$\frac{F^a}{e^{\alpha F}} \frac{R^b}{e^{\beta R}} = k.$$

Note that $\ln k$ is the constant of integration. But since k does not depend upon time, it is uniquely determined by any point (e.g., the initial points) on the trajectory. Thus if at $t = 0$, $R(0) = R_0$ and $F(0) = F_0$ then for all future time

$$k = \frac{F_0^a \quad R_0^b}{e^{\alpha F_0} \quad e^{\beta R_0}} \; .$$

Although we now know the form of the complete solution, it is a bit hard to interpret. To help do so, define

$$\Lambda(R) = R^b/\exp\{\beta R\}$$

$$\Theta(F) = F^a/\exp\{\alpha F\}.$$

Thus the complete solution is given by $\Lambda(R)\Theta(F) = k$, where $k = \Lambda(R_0) \; \Theta \; (F_0)$.

Next, look carefully at $\Lambda(R)$:

$\Lambda = 0$ when $R = 0$

$\Lambda \to 0$ as $R \to \infty$

$\dfrac{d\Lambda}{dR} = (b - \beta R)R^{b-1} \; e^{\beta R} = 0 \to \Lambda(b/\beta)$ is a maximum.

Thus, independent of the initial conditions, $\Lambda(R)$ vs. R looks like:

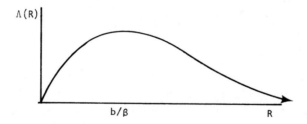

Obviously, $\Theta(F)$ looks the same.

Let us now try to work out what the Trajectory in population space (i.e. R,F space) looks like. Assume we are given the point (R_0, F_0) as the initial population configuration. This fixes the value of k. For any other value of F there will be one value of $\Theta(F)$. But since $\Lambda(R)\Theta(F) = k$, this determines the value of $\Lambda(R)$. As is clear from the figure above, associated with any value of $\Lambda(R)$ there are either two values of R or else none. One can now repeat

this argument word for word, switching R with F and Λ(R)
with Θ(F). This implies that the path in (R,F) space is a
closed loop. The rather complicated plot below may help in
visualizing the construction of population trajectories.

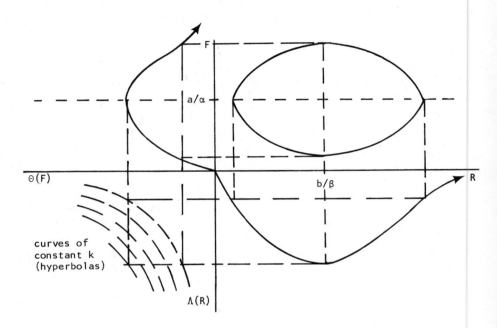

It is apparent from the shape of the Λ(R) and Θ(F)
curves that for trajectories far from the point (b/β,a/α),
the ellipses predicted by the Stability Analysis become
more and more distorted.

Comments:

1. Imagine that we start looking at a population
   cycle like the one shown in the figure, at
   the point where there are excess rabbits, but
   the foxes are in equilibrium. This condition
   makes for good hunting for the foxes, so
   their population grows at the expense of the
   rabbit population size. Finally, the rabbit

population reaches its equilibrium size, but there are too many foxes, who continue to hunt rabbits. But with too few rabbits to support them, the foxes begin to die off from starvation which lessens the pressure on the rabbit population. Finally, a low point in the rabbit population size is reached as the fox population passes again through its equilibrium size. But with the rabbit population depleted, the foxes continue to die off, thereby reducing the pressure on the rabbit population, which begins to recover, etc.

2. It is not hard to show that the trajectories in (R,F) space can not cross. Look at the D.E. whose solution is shown in the figure.

$$\frac{dR}{dF} = \frac{(a - \alpha F)R}{(-b + \beta R)F} \ .$$

At any point in (R,F) space, all the quantities on right hand side of equation are known, thus the slope in (R,F) space is uniquely determined. Therefore, trajectories can not cross, as this would require two (or more) slopes at a single point.

3. It is also not difficult to determine the average sizes of the populations over a complete cycle. For example, start with the non-linear governing equation for the rabbits

$$\frac{dR}{dt} = (a - \alpha F)R.$$

Thus over one complete cycle which takes time T

$$\int_{R(0)}^{R(T)} dR/R = \int_{0}^{T} (a - \alpha F)dt$$

$$\ln R(T) - \ln R(0) = aT - \alpha \int_0^T F\,dt = aT - \alpha \overline{F}T.$$

But, $R(T) = R(0)$, thus $\overline{F} = a/\alpha$ (similarly, $\overline{R} = b/\beta$).

This means that the average population size is the same as the equilibrium population size. Recalling the earlier observation that the elliptical orbits are quite distorted far from $(b/\beta, a/\alpha)$ implies that the speed at which populations move on trajectories is not constant.

Isoclines and Arrows: One additional method exists which is useful for determining the population space trajectory of complicated D.E.s. The idea is to plot the isoclines of the D.E.s and then to indicate by small arrows, the direction of population growth. This method is illustrated below for the Predator-Prey Equations:

$$\frac{dR}{dt} = R(a - \alpha F)$$

$$\frac{dF}{dt} = -F(b - \beta R).$$

Clearly, the isocline dR/dt = 0 must be crossed in a vertical direction, since along the isocline, the rabbit population is not changing. We could make a similar statement for dF/dt = 0.

In the figure below, we plot dR/dt = 0 and dF/dt = 0. Their points of intersection are the equilibrium points for the system. We also indicate the regions where dR/dt > 0 and dF/dt > 0. From these facts we are able to deduce the direction of the arrows shown.

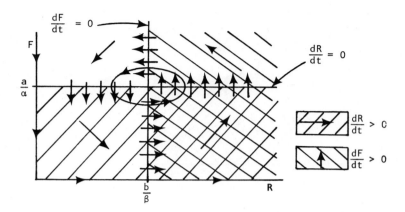

The oval shown is one of an infinite number of possible trajectories which can be deduced from the allowable directions of motion in the population plane. Note that the fact that the oval 'closes upon itself' does not follow immediately from the information available from the isoclines and arrows. It is conceivable based upon the information provided that the oval is actually a spiral which slowly expands or contracts.

We next look at a more complicated Predator-Prey interaction; one involving a carrying capacity for the Prey species. Instead of writing down the governing equations, we proceed graphically using isoclines and arrows.

The isocline dF/dt = 0 will continue to be a vertical line located at R = b/β. The isocline dR/dt = 0 will now be represented by a curve which intersects the R axis at two points, corresponding to the minimum viable density and carrying capacity (in the absence of Predators). Further, beyond some level of F, even for intermediate levels of R, dR/dt < 0.

These arguments lead to the figure shown below:

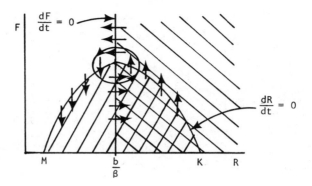

As shown, the population space trajectory is more or less as for the simple model. However, it has been inno-cently assumed that the equilibrium point occurs at the maximum point of dR/dt = 0. This certainly need not be the case as shown below.

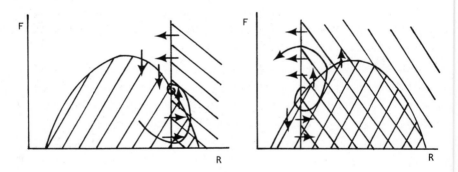

Notice that the figure on the left represents a stable configuration with the population asymptotically approaching the equilibrium point (at the intersection of the isoclines) while the figure on the right represents an unstable config-uration.

The unstable case is typical of what happens if one attempts to set up a laboratory experiment. Specifically,

the equilibrium point calls for a population of prey which
is so small that extinction occurs. One way to combat this
situation is to provide the prey with a 'hiding place' that
the predators can not reach. The figure below illustrates
such a situation.

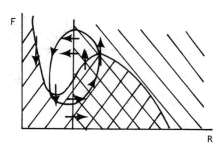

Problems

1. In 1868, the cottony cushion scale insect was acciden-
    tally introduced to the United States from Australia.
    This insect nearly destroyed the California citrus in-
    dustry. To combat the outbreak of the scale insect
    population, the natural predator, the ladybird beetle
    was also imported. The simplest equations appropriate
    to this ecosystem are:

    $$\frac{dS}{dt} = S(a - AL)$$
    $$\frac{dL}{dt} = -L(b - BS)$$

    a, A, b, B positive constants

    where S and L are the densities of scale insects and
    ladybird beetles respectively. Find the equilibrium
    population densities.

    Next, consider the effect of the introduction of
    DDT to the ecosystem. To do so, assume that the DDT
    kill rate, k, is the same for both species. Modify the
    equations to take the presence of DDT into account by
    adding a term to each equation. Then find the new

equilibrium population densities, and compare these to the pre-DDT equilibria. State in words and with a simple graph what has happened.

2. A more realistic form for predator-prey interactions takes into account the fact that the prey population, in the absence of any predators, experiences density (i.e. Logistic like) effects. Write down a new equation for the prey species along with the old predator equation, starting from the rabbit/fox model considered in class.

   a. Find all equilibrium population sizes (you should find three, two of which have the predator absent).
   b. For the one equilibrium population size with both predator and prey present, determine the stability of the system.

References

The model discussed in this section is one of the classics of population mathematics. Treatments of the analysis can be found in most texts on the subject. Two useful references are:

Kemeny, J.G. and J.L. Snell, Mathematical Models in the Social Sciences, MIT Press, Cambridge, MA, 1972.

In Chapter 3 of this undergraduate mathematics textbook, the analytic treatment of the simple predator-prey model can be found. (Note that this book was originally published in 1962 by the Blaisdell Publishing Company)

Wilson, E.O. and W.H. Bossert, A Primer of Population Biology, Sinauer Associates, Stamford, CT., 1971.

In Chapter 3 (pp. 129-138) the graphical method presented in the latter portion of this section of this monograph is developed in detail.

8 Competition and Mutualism

Frequently, when two very similar species compete with one another for limited resources (food, territory, ...) one of the two ultimately drops out of the competition. Ordinarily, this takes place by having one of the species become locally extinct. The explanation of this phenomenon, which will be developed analytically and graphically, is usually called the Principle of Competitive Exclusion, or Gause's Principle.

Consider two species, counted by X and Y, which live in direct competition with one another. Further, assume that in the absence of Y, X is limited by a carrying capacity, thus

$$r_X(X,0) = a - AX.$$

Similarly,

$$r_Y(0,Y) = b - BY.$$

In addition, since the two species compete for limited resources, the presence of each has an inhibiting effect upon the growth of the other. We represent this by the intrinsic rates

$$r_X(X,Y) = a - AX - \alpha Y$$

$$r_Y(X,Y) = b - BY - \beta X.$$

The governing equations for the two species are therefore

$$\left.\begin{aligned}\frac{dX}{dt} &= X\, r_X(X,Y) = (a - AX - \alpha Y)X \\ \frac{dY}{dt} &= Y\, r_Y(X,Y) = (b - BY - \beta X)Y\end{aligned}\right\} \quad a,b,A,B,\alpha,\beta > 0.$$

Unfortunately, these equations can not be solved directly. They are however amenable to both linearized stability analysis and also to graphical analysis.

Linearized Stability Analysis:

Equilibrium: Set $\frac{dX}{dt} = 0$ and $\frac{dY}{dt} = 0$ to get 4 Equilibrium points.

3 are trivial: $\begin{bmatrix}X = 0 \\ Y = 0\end{bmatrix}\begin{bmatrix}X = 0 \\ Y = b/B\end{bmatrix}\begin{bmatrix}X = a/A \\ Y = 0\end{bmatrix}.$

The fourth comes from solving the pair of equations:

$$\left.\begin{aligned}AX + \alpha Y &= a \\ \beta X + bY &= b\end{aligned}\right\} \rightarrow \begin{bmatrix}X = X^* = (aB - \alpha b)/(AB - \alpha\beta) \\ Y = Y^* = (Ab - a\beta)/(AB - \alpha\beta).\end{bmatrix}$$

Stability: It is not difficult to show that the equilibrium at $(0,0)$ is unstable, while the ones at $(0,b/B)$ and $(a/A,0)$ are stable.

We now consider the stability of the equilibrium at (X^*,Y^*). To do so, expand the two populations about their equilibrium points by substituting

$$\left.\begin{aligned}X &= X^*(1 + x) \\ X &= Y^*(1 + y)\end{aligned}\right\} \quad |x|,|y| \ll 1.$$

Linearizing yields

$$\frac{dx}{dt} = -AX^*x - \alpha Y^*y$$

$$\frac{dy}{dt} = -BY^*y - \beta X^*x .$$

Next, rewrite the linearized equations in matrix form

$$\begin{Bmatrix} \dot{x} \\ \dot{y} \end{Bmatrix} = \begin{pmatrix} -AX^* & -\alpha Y^* \\ -\beta X^* & -BY^* \end{pmatrix} \begin{Bmatrix} x \\ y \end{Bmatrix} \quad : \quad (\dot{\ }) = \frac{d}{dt} .$$

Assume

$$\begin{Bmatrix} x \\ y \end{Bmatrix} = \begin{Bmatrix} x_o \\ y_o \end{Bmatrix} \exp\{\lambda t\}$$

which leads to

$$\det \begin{pmatrix} -AX^* - \lambda & -\alpha Y^* \\ & \\ -\beta X^* & -BY^* - \lambda \end{pmatrix} = 0.$$

Expanding the determinant leads to the Characteristic Equation

$$\lambda^2 + (AX^* + BY^*)\lambda + (AB - \alpha\beta)X^*Y^* = 0.$$

Thus

$$\lambda_{\frac{1}{2}} = \tfrac{1}{2}\{-(AX^* + BY^*)$$

$$\pm \sqrt{(AX^* + BY^*)^2 - 4(AB - \alpha\beta)X^*Y^*}\}.$$

This expression is not as difficult to interpret as it might at first appear to be. As is always the case for the roots of a quadratic equation, there are just two distinct possibilities:

   1. The roots are complex conjugates. When this happens the solution is oscillatory in nature.

2. The roots are both real, and for this example, are equidistant from the point $-\frac{1}{2}(AX^* + BY^*)$. When this happens the solution is non-oscillatory.

Whether 1. or 2. is the case depends upon the sign of the discriminant (i.e. the term under the square root.) By plotting the locus of the roots in the complex λ plane, it becomes easy to decide what we wish to know.

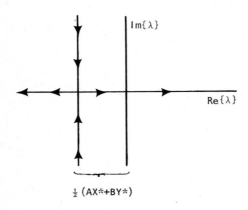

$\frac{1}{2}(AX*+BY*)$

Vertical arrows: discriminant < 0.

Double root: discriminant = 0.

Horizontal arrows: discriminant > 0.

Notice that the oscillatory roots are always stable. Also, the transition from stable to unstable equilibrium occurs when $\lambda_1 = 0$. Clearly, this happens when

$$\sqrt{(AX^* + BY^*)^2 - 4(AB - \alpha\beta)X^*Y^*} = (AX^* + BY^*).$$

This obviously occurs when $AB = \alpha\beta$.

In addition, $AB > \alpha\beta \rightarrow$ Stable
                  $AB < \alpha\beta \rightarrow$ Unstable.

Let us interpret this result biologically. By referring back to the original equations, it is apparent that

1. A and B measure 'self-regulation'
2. α and β measure 'interspecies competition'.

We have found that the co-existence of the two competing

species is unstable if the species compete so strongly that they tend to regulate one another's growth more strongly than they tend to regulate their own growth. The idea that strongly competing species can not stably cohabit is often referred to as the Principle of Competitive Exclusion or Gause's Principle.

Instead of trying to carry the linearized stability analysis any farther, we will next use the method of isoclines and arrows to determine the nature of the trajectories in 'population space'. Referring to the original equations, it is easy to see that

$$\frac{dX}{dt} = 0 \text{ along lines } X = 0 \text{ and } AX + \alpha Y = a$$

$$\frac{dY}{dt} = 0 \text{ along lines } Y = 0 \text{ and } \beta X + BY = b.$$

Notice that the two lines which are not the axes have intercepts

$$(0, a/\alpha) \text{ and } (a/A, 0)$$
$$(0, b/B) \text{ and } (b/\beta, 0)$$

Clearly, there are four distinct situations which depend upon the relative size of a/A, a/α, b/B, b/β. These are now illustrated.

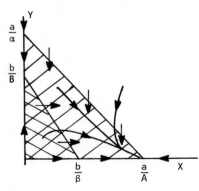

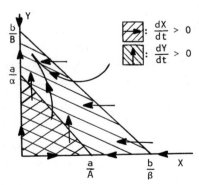

Case 1:

$$\frac{a}{A} > \frac{b}{\beta} \text{ and } \frac{a}{\alpha} > \frac{b}{B} .$$

End up at $(a/A, 0)$, regardless of where population starts.

Case 2:

$$\frac{a}{A} < \frac{b}{\beta} \text{ and } \frac{a}{\alpha} < \frac{b}{B} .$$

End up at $(0, b/B)$, regardless of where population starts.

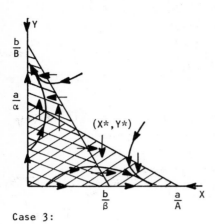

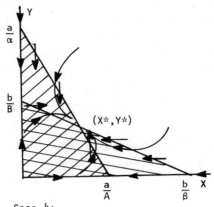

Case 3:

$$\frac{a}{A} > \frac{b}{\beta} \text{ and } \frac{a}{\alpha} < \frac{b}{B} \rightarrow AB > \alpha\beta.$$

End up at (a/A,0) or (0,b/B),
depending on initial population.

Case 4:

$$\frac{a}{A} < \frac{b}{\beta} \text{ and } \frac{a}{\alpha} > \frac{b}{B} \rightarrow AB < \alpha\beta.$$

End up at (X*,Y*), regardless of
where population starts.

The last two cases illustrate the Principle of Competitive
Exclusion.

Mutualism: Sometimes, two species interact with one another
in such a fashion that each, by its presence, tends to ben-
efit the other. A simple example of such an ecosystem is
one composed of a plant species and a pollinator insect,
where the pollen serves as the source of food for the insect. If the ecosystem requires the presence of both
species to avoid extinction of both, the interaction is
called 'obligate' mutualism.

Historically, mutualism has received much less interest than predator-prey and competition for two reasons:

      1. The simple analog of the (quadratically non-
           linear) predator-prey or competition models
           leads to silly results - usually, both species
           grow without bound.

2. Outside of the humid tropics, mutualistic
    interactions do not tend to be found. Re-
    cently, studies of mutualistic interactions
    have received considerable attention.

We could easily convert the equations which we derived
for competitive interaction so that they describe mutualistic interaction. Using the basic idea that the presence of
each species benefits the other leads to the set of equations for the plants P and insects I:

$$\left. \begin{aligned} \frac{dP}{dt} &= P(a - AP + \alpha I) \\ \frac{dI}{dt} &= I(b - BI + \beta P) \end{aligned} \right\} \quad a,b,A,B,\alpha,\beta > 0.$$

But as noted above, these equations lead to the conclusion
that in the presence of strong mutualism, both species grow
without bound, even though each species is limited by a
carrying capacity in the absence of the other species.

We therefore proceed directly to another form of the
equations. Instead of considering the presence of each
species to increase the growth rate of the other species,
we will allow the presence of each species to increase the
carrying capacity of the other species. This causes our
equations to assume the form

$$\left. \begin{aligned} \frac{dP}{dt} &= rP\left[1 - P/(K + \alpha I)\right] \\ \frac{dI}{dt} &= rI\left[1 - I/(H + \beta P)\right] \end{aligned} \right\} \quad r,K,H,\alpha,\beta > 0$$

where K and H are the carrying capacities of the environment for the plants and insects respectively, each in the
absence of the other, α and β are coefficients which measure the influence of the presence of insects and plants,
respectively, upon the carrying capacities of each other,
and r is a growth rate factor which has been assumed to be
the same for the two species (to avoid unnecessary confusion
which easily results from the proliferation of coefficients.)

In addition to the three trivial equilibria (both species absent, and two with one species absent and the other at its carrying capacity K or H respectively) there is an equilibrium with both species present. The equilibrium is located at

$$P = P^* = (K + \alpha H)/(1 - \alpha\beta) > K$$

$$I = I^* = (H + \beta K)/(1 - \alpha\beta) > H.$$

Notice that to avoid meaningless results, we must demand that $\alpha\beta < 1$.

Stability: We could determine the stability of the equilibrium at the point (P^*, I^*) by expanding the governing D.E.s and linearizing; however, this would lead to an awful mess. Let us therefore proceed formally to develop a modified technique for doing stability analyses. To do so, rewrite the governing D.E.s

$$\left. \begin{array}{l} \dfrac{dP}{dt} = f(P,I) \\[2ex] \dfrac{dI}{dt} = g(P,I) \end{array} \right\} : \left\{ \begin{array}{l} f(P,I) = rP\left[1 - P/(K + \alpha I)\right] \\[2ex] g(P,I) = rI\left[1 - I/(H + \beta P)\right] \end{array} \right.$$

and define the disturbance from equilibrium to be

$$P(t) = P^* + \xi(t)$$

$$I(t) = I^* + \eta(t).$$

Substituting the disturbance terms into the D.E.s then leads to

$$\frac{d\xi}{dt} = f(P^* + \xi, I^* + \eta)$$

$$\frac{d\eta}{dt} = g(P^* + \xi, I^* + \eta).$$

But the expressions on the right hand sides of the equations are just the Taylor Series expansions of $f(P,I)$ and $g(P,I)$ about the equilibrium point (P^*, I^*).

Digression: Taylor Series expansion of a function of two
            variables: (n.b. to avoid confusion, we use
            new variable names in the digression.)

Given a function of two variables, $w = z(x,y)$, approximate w by its Taylor Series expansion near the point (a,b).
In other words, find the value of the function at the point
$(a+h,b+k)$ in terms of its value and those of its derivatives at the point (a,b).

Define:
$$x = a + hs$$
$$y = b + ks$$

and let
$$Z(s) = z(x,y) = z(a + hs, b + ks).$$

Notice that
$$Z(0) = z(a,b)$$
$$Z(1) = z(a + h, b + k).$$

But $Z(s)$ is now a function of one variable, hence its Taylor Series expansion about the point $s = 0$ is known to be

$$Z(s) = Z(0) + \frac{dZ}{ds}\bigg|_{s=0} s + \frac{1}{2!} \frac{d^2Z}{ds^2}\bigg|_{s=0} s^2 + \cdots$$

But
$$\frac{dZ}{ds}\bigg|_{s=0} = \frac{d}{ds}\left[z(x,y)\right]\bigg|_{s=0} = \left[\frac{\partial z}{\partial x}\frac{dx}{ds} + \frac{\partial z}{\partial y}\frac{dy}{ds}\right]\bigg|_{\substack{x=a\\y=b}}$$

$$= \left[h\frac{\partial z}{\partial x} + k\frac{\partial z}{\partial y}\right]\bigg|_{\substack{x=a\\y=b}}$$

and a similar procedure leads to the higher derivatives.
Thus by setting $s = 1$ in the expression for $Z(s)$, we arrive
at

$$Z(1) = Z(0) + \frac{dZ}{ds}\bigg|_{s=0} + \frac{1}{2}\frac{d^2Z}{ds^2}\bigg|_{s=0} + \cdots$$

$$z(a + h, b + k) = z(a,b) + \left[h\frac{\partial z}{\partial x} + k\frac{\partial z}{\partial y}\right]\bigg|_{\substack{x=a\\y=b}} + \cdots$$

Returning now to our stability analysis, it is not hard

to see that up to first order terms in ξ and η, the D.E.s become

$$\frac{d\xi}{dt} = \xi\frac{\partial f}{\partial P}\Big|_* + \eta\frac{\partial f}{\partial I}\Big|_*$$

$$(\cdot)\Big|_* = (\cdot)\Big|_{\substack{P=P^*_* \\ I=I^*}} .$$

$$\frac{d\eta}{dt} = \xi\frac{\partial g}{\partial P}\Big|_* + \eta\frac{\partial g}{\partial I}\Big|_*$$

Note that the constant terms on the right hand side have dropped out (as they always will) since due to equilibrium, $f(P^*,I^*) = g(P^*,I^*) = 0$.

By evaluating the partial derivatives of f and g we find the D.E.s

$$\frac{d\xi}{dt} = -r\xi + \alpha r\eta$$

$$\frac{d\eta}{dt} = \beta r\xi - r\eta.$$

The associated Characteristic Equation for the roots is then

$$\lambda^2 + 2r\lambda + r^2(1 - \alpha\beta) = 0.$$

Thus $\quad \lambda_{\frac{1}{2}} = -r\left[1 \pm \sqrt{\alpha\beta}\,\right].$

Since on physical grounds we demand that $\alpha\beta < 1$, it follows that the equilibrium at (P^*,I^*) is always stable.

Characteristic Return Time: If a system is disturbed away from its equilibrium point, and if it is stable, the rate at which it returns to equilibrium is governed by the magnitude of the real part of the root of the Characteristic Equation with the largest real part. It is customary to refer to the reciprocal of this quantity as the Characteristic Return Time, T_R.

If the two populations under study show no mutualistic interaction (i.e. $\alpha = \beta = 0$) then $T_R = 1/r$, while with mutualism, $T_R = 1/r\left[1 - \sqrt{\alpha\beta}\,\right]$. In other words, when mutualistic effects occur, the system returns to equilibrium more slowly than when mutualistic effects are absent.

We next look at the more complicated model which describes obligate mutualism. We will do this graphically, never actually writing down the complete equations. We make two assumptions.

1. The insects' sole source of food is the nectar from the plants. Thus, in the absence of plants, the carrying capacity for the insects (previously called H) goes to zero.

2. The plants are outcrossers (i.e. not self-pollinating). When plants are scarce, not only does natural pollination drop off, but also the insects find it hard to find more than one plant (which is necessary if pollination is to occur).

We plot below on the left, the isoclines and arrows for the system studied previously, and on the right, the obligate system.

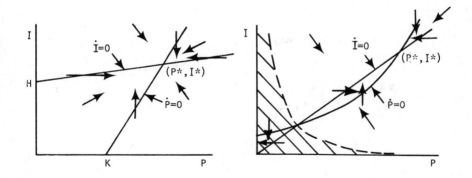

Notice that in going to the obligate system, the insect isocline was rotated so that it passes through the origin, and the plant isocline was bent to account for the fact that at low plant density, greater insect density is needed just to maintain the population of plants at a fixed size. The result is that an unstable equilibrium point develops. For any initial population point within the cross-hatched region, ultimate extinction will occur.

If we permit ourselves to visualize what happens if there is some amount of fluctuation in the environmental conditions, we conclude that it is likely that the obligate system will eventually be swept into the cross-hatched region, from which point extinction is rather probable. This helps to explain why obligate mutualistic ecosystems do not tend to occur outside of the very constant environmental conditions which occur in the humid tropics.

Problems

1. The simplest model for the competitive interaction of two species is given by the equations

$$\left.\begin{array}{l} \dfrac{dX}{dt} = X(a - \alpha Y) \\[2mm] \dfrac{dY}{dt} = Y(b - \beta X) \end{array}\right\} \quad a,b,\alpha,\beta > 0.$$

   a. Find all equilibrium points and determine the stability at any which have both species present.

   b. Show that the linearized approximation to the solution in 'population space' is a family of hyperbolas.

   c. Use the method of isoclines and arrows on the original equations to sketch the solution for a variety of initial populations.

2. A proposal model for mutualism is of the form

$$\left.\begin{array}{l} \dfrac{dX}{dt} = X(a - AX + \alpha Y) \\[2mm] \dfrac{dY}{dt} = Y(b - BY + \beta X) \end{array}\right\} \quad a,b,A,B,\alpha,\beta > 0.$$

Determine the relative sizes of the parameters if the system is not to admit the pathological situation where mutualism leads to unbounded growth.

References

An extensive literature exists on the subject of competition. Several references, both biological and mathematical, are listed below. Far less has been written about mutualism; for some speculation as to the reason for this imbalance, see R.M. May.

Gause, G.F., The Struggle for Existence, Hafner, New York 1964.

This book is the classical tome on competition, and includes data as well as mathematics. The book was originally published in 1934 by Williams and Wilkins, Baltimore, MD.

May, R.M., "Models for Two Interacting Populations", Chapter 4 of Theoretical Ecology, Principles and Applications, R.M. May (ed), Saunders Co., Philadelphia, PA, 1976.

In section 4.3 competition is discussed, though some of the treatment is beyond the scope of this monograph. (By all means, do not miss the rhyme about niches by Dr. Seuss which is quoted on page 59.) The material in section 4.4 on mutualism is interesting, and offers further references to the literature.

Wilson, E.O. and W.H. Bossert, A Primer of Population Biology, Sinauer Associates, Stamford, CT, 1971.

On pp. 156-164, competition is discussed in lucid, biological terms, with extensive graphical illustration.

9 Quadratic Two-Species Population Models

We proceed now to look at a rather general model for the interaction of two biological species. Special cases of this model will represent Predator-Prey, Competitive and Mutualistic interactions. We will however be able to demonstrate a very general result for all such models. Specifically, we will show that the models almost never admit periodic (cyclic) solutions. This of course means that in terms of finding a model which describes an ecosystem which is known to behave in a cyclic manner, the model discussed below is not adequate.

We describe the population of the two species at time t by $x(t)$ and $y(t)$, and incorporate coefficients to model density independent growth rates (a_0 and b_0), self-regulatory effects (a_1 and b_2) and also cross-regulatory effects (a_2 and b_1). The model, which we will call the two-species, quadratic population growth model is then

$$\frac{dx}{dt} = f(x,y) = x(a_0 + a_1 x + a_2 y)$$

$$\frac{dy}{dt} = g(x,y) = y(b_0 + b_1 x + b_2 y).$$

Note that we have <u>not</u> specified the sign of the a's and b's. To get the special cases which we have studied already, we make the following specifications:

Predator-Prey: $\quad a_0 > 0 \quad a_1 \leq 0 \quad a_2 < 0$

$\qquad\qquad\qquad\quad b_0 < 0 \quad b_1 > 0 \quad b_2 \leq 0.$

N.B. The Lotka-Volterra model results if we choose $a_1 = b_2 = 0.$

Competition: $\quad a_0 > 0 \quad a_1 < 0 \quad a_2 < 0$

$\qquad\qquad\qquad b_0 > 0 \quad b_1 < 0 \quad b_2 < 0.$

Mutualism: $\quad a_0 > 0 \quad a_1 < 0 \quad a_2 > 0$

$\qquad\qquad\qquad b_0 > 0 \quad b_1 > 0 \quad b_2 < 0.$

We continue our investigation now for the general model with the a's and b's unspecified. We will develop conditions as we need them on the a's and b's.

Equilibrium: There are four equilibrium points, three of which we regard as 'trivial' as they have one or both species absent. The one equilibrium which interests us is the one at

$$x = x^* = \frac{a_2 b_0 - a_0 b_2}{a_1 b_2 - a_2 b_1}, \quad y = y^* = \frac{a_0 b_1 - a_1 b_0}{a_1 b_2 - a_2 b_1}.$$

Clearly, the first condition which we must specify is that $a_1 b_2 \neq a_2 b_1$ so as to keep x^* and y^* finite.

N.B. for physical reasons, we also want $x^* > 0$ and $y^* > 0$.

If the equilibrium is stable, then $x(t) = x^*$ and $y(t) = y^*$ for all t. Another type of equilibrium is also conceivable. Specifically, it may happen that $x(t)$ and $y(t)$ do not remain constant, but rather fluctuate in a periodic manner. In population space, this would be represented by an orbit which is usually called a cycle.

Ordinarily, at this point, we would linearize the equations about the equilibrium point to assess the stability.

But this might cause us to overlook (i.e. to throw away)
the cyclic solutions. We therefore will proceed without
linearizing. What we will show is that even the full quadratically non-linear D.E.s admit <u>almost</u> <u>no</u> cyclic solutions.
(We will explain "almost no" later.)

We start by stating two conditions:

Condition A: The number $A = a_1 b_2 - a_2 b_1 \neq 0$.

Condition B: The number $B = a_1 b_0 (a_2 - b_2)$

$$- a_0 b_2 (a_1 - b_1) \neq 0.$$

We have seen Condition A before. Recall that it guarantees
that the equilibrium at (x^*, y^*) is finite. To say this
another way, it asserts that the two lines

$$\left. \begin{array}{l} a_0 + a_1 x + a_2 y = C_1 \\[2mm] b_0 + b_1 x + b_2 y = C_2 \end{array} \right\} : C_1, C_2 \text{ constants}$$

are not parallel.

Condition B does not have such a simple physical interpretation. However, if it is violated, if there are
any cyclic solutions at all, then there are a continous band
of such cyclic solutions. Note that for any real ecosystem,
we would expect that the a's and b's are only approximate
(and probably change slightly over time); thus to have $B = 0$
is not realistic.

We now make an assertion which we will subsequently
prove. If the coefficients of the quadratic population
model satisfy Conditions A and B, then no cyclic solutions
can occur in population space.

Our proof proceeds as follows. Define the function

$$K(x,y) = x^\alpha y^\beta : x > 0, y > 0$$

where $\qquad \alpha = \dfrac{b_2 (b_1 - a_1)}{A} - 1 , \quad \beta = \dfrac{a_1 (a_2 - b_2)}{A} - 1.$

Assume that the quadratic population model

$$\frac{dx}{dt} = f(x,y), \frac{dy}{dt} = g(x,y)$$

has a periodic solution which is represented by the orbit Γ in population space. Also, call the region which includes Γ and its interior, R. Clearly, since Γ is a closed curve, it has an interior.

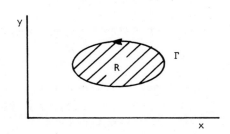

Lemma 1: Since Γ is a solution to the quadratic population model, along Γ.

$$\frac{dx}{dt} = f(x,y), \frac{dy}{dt} = g(x,y)$$

Thus:

$$\oint_{\Gamma} [Kg \ dx - Kf \ dy] = \int_{0}^{T} [Kg \frac{dx}{dt} - Kf \frac{dy}{dt}] \ dt$$

$$= \int_{0}^{T} [Kgf - Kfg] \ dt = 0$$

where T is the period of the cycle Γ.

Lemma 2: It is easily shown that:

$$\frac{\partial}{\partial x} (Kf) + \frac{\partial}{\partial y} (Kg) = \frac{B}{A} K$$

whether or not B = 0, so long as A $\neq$ 0.

Our proof proceeds as follows. Since $K(x,y) > 0$ when $x > 0$ and $y > 0$, and since A and B are non-zero constants by Conditions A and B, it follows that the quantity

$(B/A)K(x,y)$ has a fixed sign everywhere in population space. We assume $(B/A)K(x,y) > 0$. (The other case is treated in a similar manner.) It therefore follows that

$$\int\int_R \frac{B}{A} K(x,y) \ dx \ dy \ > \ 0.$$

Thus by Lemma 2:

$$\int\int_R \left[\frac{\partial}{\partial x} (Kf) + \frac{\partial}{\partial y} (Kg)\right] dx \ dy \ > \ 0.$$

We now apply Green's Theorem in the plane to replace the double integral over R by a line integral around Γ:

$$0 \ < \ \int\int_R \left[\frac{\partial}{\partial x} (Kf) + \frac{\partial}{\partial y} (Kg)\right] dx \ dy$$

$$= \ \oint_\Gamma [Kg \ dx - Kf \ dy] = 0$$

where the final equality to zero follows from Lemma 1.

But the bottom line is a contradiction. It therefore follows that Γ is not a (cyclic) solution of the quadratic population model. QED

This of course means that when Conditions A and B are satisfied (as we agreed in reality they must be,) the quadratic population model has as its only non-trivial equilibrium state the one given by $x(t) = x^*$, $y(t) = y^*$.

We next attempt to reconcile our earlier finding that the full non-linear solution to the Lotka-Volterra Equations is represented by cycles in population space. In fact, recall that we found that the L-V equations admitted not one, but rather a continuous band of cycles.

The Lotka-Volterra Equations are given by:

$$\frac{dR}{dt} = R(a - \alpha F) \left.\right\}$$
$$\frac{dF}{dt} = F(-b + \beta R) \left.\right\} \quad a,b,\alpha,\beta > 0.$$

The correspondence with our generic form for the quadratic population model is then given by:

$$\{x,y,a_0,a_1,a_2,b_0,b_1,b_2\} \rightleftharpoons \{R,F,a,0,-\alpha,-b,\beta,0\}.$$

In view of the observation that no cyclic solutions can occur if Conditions A and B are satisfied, one or the other (or both) must be violated.

$A = 0 \cdot 0 - (-\alpha) \cdot \beta = \alpha\beta \neq 0$ (Condition A satisfied)

$B = 0 \cdot (-b) \cdot (-\alpha-0) - a \cdot 0 \cdot (0-\beta) = 0$

(Condition B violated)

We are now in a position to understand why the L-V Model is not a good description of Predator-Prey inter-actions. To do this, we will extend our conception of stability. In anticipation, note that whenever either Con-dition A or B (or both) is violated, if there is any cycle at all, then there is a continuous family of cycles in pop-ulation space. In other words, under these circumstances, we would not find a single, isolated cycle.

Stability: In the real world, the trajectory which charac-terizes a biological system will inevitably be 'knocked about' a little, due to features of the world which are not included in our model. But if a cyclic trajectory perseveres over any reasonable period of time, it must be insensi-tive to such disturbances. Thus, if the system is disturbed from its trajectory, it must tend to return. This type of stability is usually called 'ecological stability', or in mathemati-cal parlance, asymptotic orbital stability.

In a sense, it is just a 'dynamic' analog of
our usual conception of stability in which we
demand that for an equilibrium point to be
stable, small disturbances must die away as
time passes, if the system is to be found at
the equilibrium point.

The figure below illustrates an ecologically stable system.
Γ is a cyclic solution to the governing equations, and P is
a point on Γ. If the system is disturbed by a small amount
to point Q, the trajectory returns asymptotically to Γ.

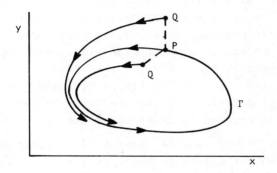

Clearly, the Lotka-Volterra Equations are <u>not</u> ecologically stable. As we have already observed, if the solution
is disturbed from one cyclic solution, it does not tend to
return, but rather follows a new orbit. If another disturbance occurs, the system follows yet another orbit.

There is another type of stability which we might reasonably expect a biological system to exhibit; 'structural
stability'. A system is called structurally stable if small
changes in the parameters do not cause the number or nature
of the equilibria to change much. We feel justified in
making this demand since the parameters are at best approximate descriptions of reality, which could well evolve in
time.

Clearly, the Lotka-Volterra Equations are <u>not</u> structurally stable. To see this, simply observe that if the parameter called a_1 in the quadratic population model (which is zero for the Lotka-Volterra Equations) was vanishingly different from zero, then Condition B would be satisfied. This of course means that the nature of the equilibrium solution changes radically as a consequence of the fact that the modifed equations can have no cyclic solutions.

As a consequence of the above observations, it is clear that the Lotka-Volterra Equations are defective. Specifically, if we persist in our belief that biological systems can exhibit persistent cycles, we must recognize that the quadratic models we have studied are simply wrong. This is true because the Lotka-Volterra Equations are neither ecologically nor structurally stable, and any other device we might contrive to make Condition B inoperative is simply too fragile, and leads to these same defects.

There are of course a few logical directions to proceed if we wish our models to admit isolated, cyclic solutions:

1. Extend models so they are cubic, or quartic, or . . .

2. Introduce discrete time lags, or even go to difference equations.

3. Allow the parameters of the equations to vary in time.

4. Introduce more species into the ecosystem.

Our discussion of quadratic population models has brought us so close to one of the significant unsolved problems of mathematical analysis that we really must digress briefly to introduce this problem.

We consider a pair of D.E.s of the general form

$$\frac{dx}{dt} = F(x,y)$$

$$\frac{dy}{dt} = G(x,y)$$

where the functions $F(x,y)$ and $G(x,y)$ are continuously differentiable in both x and y for all x and y. Further, a
solution to the equations is given by $x = x(t)$, $y = y(t)$ if
the following conditions hold:

1. $x(t)$ and $y(t)$ are defined on the common in-
    terval I: $a < t < b$; where a may be $-\infty$ and
    b may be $+\infty$.

2. $x(t)$ and $y(t)$ are continously differentiable
    and satisfy the D.E.s for all t in the inter-
    val I.

3. $x(t)$ and $y(t)$ are 'maximally extended' in
    time.

4. $x(t)$ and $y(t)$ define a curve Γ in the x-y
    plane which we call an orbit. We assume with-
    out proof that
    a. no two orbits intersect unless they
        coincide
    b. an orbit is either a non-self-
        intersecting curve, a simple closed
        curve or a single point.

In the figure below, the three possible types of
orbits are illustrated.

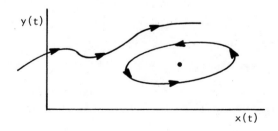

Our main interest will be in non-constant solutions such that

$$x(t) = x(t + T), \quad y(t) = y(t + T)$$

where T is called the period of the orbit. We will refer to such solutions as cycles. Notice that since $F(x,y)$ and $G(x,y)$ do not depend explicitly on time, the cyclic solutions are internally generated, as opposed to being 'imposed' upon the system.

We have already seen that by the appropriate choice of the functions $F(x,y)$ and $G(x,y)$, a variety of different types of solutions are possible. Specifically, the Lotka-Volterra equations lead to an infinite number of cycles, while the Competition, Mutualism and general Predator-Prey equations lead to no cycles at all.

It is not hard to see that the polar coordinate system

$$\frac{dr}{dt} = r(1 - r^2)(4 - r^2)\cdots(N^2 - r^2); \quad r \geq 0$$

$$\frac{d\theta}{dt} = 1$$

with N a positive integer, corresponds to the rectangular system

$$\frac{dx}{dt} = F(x,y)$$

$$\frac{dy}{dt} = G(x,y)$$

where $F(x,y)$ and $G(x,y)$ are polynomials in x and y of degree $2N + 1$. This system has a unique critical point at the origin, and N isolated cycles corresponding to the circles

$$r = 1, \quad r = 2, \quad \ldots, \quad r = N$$

and no non-isolated cycles.

Hilbert's 16th Problem: What is the maximum number of cycles $H(n)$ for the system of differential equations under

study, if F(x,y) and/or G(x,y) are 'rational integral functions' of degree n in x and y?

N.B. 'Rational integral functions' are polynomials of the
form

$$a_{00} + a_{10}x + a_{01}y + a_{20}x^2 + a_{11}xy + \cdots + a_{0n}y^n.$$

We call H(n) the Hilbert Function, and consider only isolated cycles.

It is not hard to show that H(0) = 0 and H(1) = 0. We
also have from the above example that for each <u>odd</u> integer
n = 2N + 1, H(n) $\geq$ N.

In 1939, the Soviet mathematician N.N. Bautin announced
the result:

H(2) $\geq$ 3, and no more than 3 isolated cycles can
enclose a given critical point when n = 2.

N.B. The system with n = 2 can have more than one critical
point. Although this implies that H(2) might be
greater than 3, many feel that H(2) = 3.

In the mid-1950's a pair of papers by Petrovsky and
Landis 'proved' that H(2) = 3, and that for n > 2

$$H(n) \leq \begin{cases} \frac{1}{2}(6n^3 - 7n^2 - 11n + 6); \text{ n odd} \\ \frac{1}{2}(6n^3 - 7n^2 + n + 4); \text{ n even.} \end{cases}$$

Unfortunately, these papers contain a flaw which renders
this result tentative as opposed to proven. Even without
the result H(2) = 3, it can be shown that when n = 2, every
cycle is convex, and contains just one critical point in its
interior. Further, cycles enclosing the same critical point
have the same orientation (in time) while those enclosing
another critical point have opposite orientation.

This represents the present state of knowledge re-
garding H(n).

1. Verify Lemma 2.

2. Consider the following system of equations:

$$\frac{dx}{dt} = x(1 - x^2 - y^2) - y$$

$$\frac{dy}{dt} = y(1 - x^2 - y^2) + x.$$

Note that this is not a model for two species interaction; hence relax the usual restriction that $x > 0$, $y > 0$. Note also that the equations are cubic, not quadratic.

     a.   Locate the equilibrium point.

     b.   Determine the linearized stability at the equilibrium point.

     c.   Show that the non-linear equations admit a solution which is a single, isolated cycle. To do so, solve the equations. (Hint: use polar coordinates

$$r = (x^2 + y^2)^{\frac{1}{2}}, \quad \theta = \tan^{-1}(y/x).$$

This should lead to two decoupled equations, both of which can be solved by separation of variables.)

     d.   Sketch the solution in (x,y) space.

     e.   Compare the results of parts a and b with the results of parts c and d.

3. Show that the system

$$\frac{dx}{dt} = x \sin(x^2 + y^2) - y$$

$$\frac{dy}{dt} = y \sin(x^2 + y^2) + x$$

has infinitely many isolated cycles. (Hint: use polar coordinates.)

4. Show that $H(1) = 0$ (Hint: consider the system

$$\frac{dx}{dt} = a_1 x + a_2 y$$

$$\frac{dy}{dt} = b_1 x + b_2 y.$$

Suppose that system has solution $x_1 = x(t)$, $y_1 = y(t)$ with the orbit Γ_1. Show that $x_2 = cx(t)$, $y_2 = cy(t)$ is also a solution for any constant c, hence Γ_1 is not isolated. Then extend to case where equations also contain constants a_0 and b_0 respectively on right hand sides.

5. Solve the system of equations

$$\frac{dx}{dt} = x - 1$$

$$\frac{dy}{dt} = 2y$$

and then plot the results in (x,y) coordinates.

References

The material in this section is drawn from two teaching modules by C.S. Coleman. At the present time, these are available from:

Professor W.F. Lucas
334 Upson Hall
Cornell University
Ithaca, NY 14853

Coleman, C.S., "Hilbert's 16th Problem: How Many Cycles?", MAA Workshop on Modules in Applied Mathematics, Cornell University, 1976.

This module is extremely entertaining, and provides access to a number of unsolved problems in mathematical analysis. It is strongly recommended as an accompaniment to this section of the monograph.

Coleman, S.C., "Quadratic Population Models: Almost Never Any Cycles", MAA Workshop on Modules in Applied Mathematics, Cornell University, 1976.

As with the above module, a variety of interesting results concerning mathematical analysis are reported in an ecological context. This module is also strongly recommended.

10 Three-Species Competition

Although the quadratic population models for two species were not very satisfactory in the cases of Predator-Prey and Mutualism, in the case of Competition we discovered the well accepted Principle of Competitive Exclusion. We will therefore choose to extend the simple quadratic model of competition to include three interacting species.

Before proceeding, let us recall the nature of the results for two competing species (call them species 1 and 2). The quadratically nonlinear model resulted in four distinct equilibrium points, one with both species absent, one with species 1 only, one with species 2 only, and one with both species coexisting. The condition for stable coexistence was that intraspecies competition be stronger than interspecies competition. Recall further that under no circumstances did the system manifest periodic cycles.

We now consider three competing species (call them 1, 2 and 3.) Our model will be just a formal generalization of the two species model. We will choose to let

$N_i(t)$ = number of species i present at time t, i = 1, 2, 3.

r_i = intrinsic growth rate of species i in the absence of any (self or cross) competition.

α_{ij} = effect of presence of species j on growth of species i. (All the $\alpha_{ij} > 0$.)

In compact notation, our three species, quadratically nonlinear model then is written

$$\frac{dN_i(t)}{dt} = r_i N_i(t) \left[1 - \sum_{j=1}^{3} \alpha_{ij} N_j(t) \right] : i = 1, 2, 3.$$

Unfortunately, this system contains 12 parameters (3 r's and 9 α's). At the cost of considerable reality, we make the system manageable by reducing the number of available constants. We do this as follows:

1. $r_1 = r_2 = r_3 = r > 0$

2. $\alpha_{12} = \alpha_{23} = \alpha_{31} = \alpha > 0$

3. $\alpha_{21} = \alpha_{32} = \alpha_{13} = \beta > 0$.

Then, by rescaling time we can effectively make r = 1 and by rescaling the $N_i(t)$ we can effectively make $\alpha_{11} = \alpha_{22} = \alpha_{33} = 1$. Thus

$$\frac{dN_1}{dt} = N_1 \left[1 - N_1 - \alpha N_2 - \beta N_3 \right]$$

$$\frac{dN_2}{dt} = N_2 \left[1 - \beta N_1 - N_2 - \alpha N_3 \right]$$

$$\frac{dN_3}{dt} = N_3 \left[1 - \alpha N_1 - \beta N_2 - N_3 \right].$$

It is possible, though not certain, that the qualitative results for this highly symmetrical model will also hold for a more realistic unsymmetrical model.

Equilibrium: It is not difficult to show that there are 8 possible equilibrium points with the following physical interpretation:

One point: $(0,0,0) \rightleftarrows$ all three species absent.

Three of form: $(1,0,0) \rightleftarrows$ one species present.

Three of form: $\dfrac{(1-\alpha,\ 1-\beta,0)}{(1-\alpha\beta)} \rightleftarrows$ two species present.

One point: $\dfrac{(1,1,1)}{(1+\alpha+\beta)} \rightleftarrows$ all species present.

Stability: It is also straightforward (though algebraically messy) to assess the stability of the equilibrium points. Of particular interest to us is the result for the point with all three species present. The roots of the appropriate Characteristic Equation can be shown to be

$$\lambda_1 = -(1 + \alpha + \beta)$$
$$\lambda_{\frac{2}{3}} = -1 + \frac{(\alpha + \beta)}{2} \pm i\,(\alpha - \beta)\,\frac{\sqrt{3}}{2}.$$

It therefore follows that the equilibrium point with all three species present is locally stable if and only if $\alpha + \beta < 2$. (Recall also that $\alpha > 0$, $\beta > 0$.)

In the figure below the dynamical properties of the system are shown as functions of the two parameters α and β.

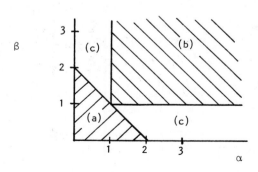

(a) Stable equilibrium with all three species present.

(b) All three of the single-species equilibrium points $(1,0,0)$, $(0,1,0)$ and $(0,0,1)$ stable; which one the system converges to depends upon initial conditions.

(c) No asymptotically stable equilibrium point exists. Instead, the system manifests cyclic behavior.

Notice that the equilibrium points with all species absent and with any two species present are never stable. This is a result of our too restrictive interpretation of extinction. For example, with regard to the case with all species absent, it only says that if we introduce some animals, they will initially thrive; it does not say that they will spontaneously appear. In a similar manner, with regard to the case with just two species present, it says that the system is unstable with respect to small disturbances which include the third (absent) species. As a result of this mathematical pathology, we must be quite careful in interpreting results.

Let us now look carefully at the situation in which $\alpha + \beta = 2$. This occurs on the diagonal line in the figure above which divides regions (a) and (c). Since this line is of measure zero, we do not really ever expect it to occur. (This is essentially the same flaw as we detected for the Lotka-Volterra Equations for Predator-Prey systems.) We study this case because it leads to interesting results which can be generalized to the case $\alpha + \beta \geq 2$, with one of α or $\beta < 1$ (i.e. to points in region (c) in the figure.)

We begin by defining

$$S(t) = N_1(t) + N_2(t) + N_3(t).$$

Next, add the three governing D.E.s using $\alpha + \beta = 2$ to get

$$\frac{dS}{dt} = S(1 - S).$$

Observe that this is just the Logistic Equation with the Carrying Capacity equal to 1 (unity). Thus

$$S(t \to \infty) \to 1.$$

Note that the equation

$$S = N_1 + N_2 + N_3 = 1$$

is just a plane in three dimensions which intersects each axis at unity as shown below.

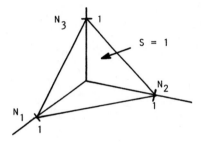

Our result tells us that after a long time, the solution will lie in the inclined plane $S = 1$.

Next, notice that the first of the D.E.'s can be written

$$\frac{d \ln N_1}{dt} = 1 - N_1 - \alpha N_2 - \beta N_3$$

and similarly for the other two equations.

Adding the three equations in this form, using $\alpha + \beta = 2$, leads to

$$\frac{d}{dt} \left[\ln (N_1 N_2 N_3) \right] = 3(1 - S).$$

Define

$$P = N_1 N_2 N_3$$

and observe from above that

$$\frac{d \ln S}{dt} = (1 - S).$$

Thus

$$\frac{d \ln P}{dt} = 3 \frac{d \ln S}{dt} .$$

Integrate both sides with respect to time from the initial point $N_1(0)$, $N_2(0)$, $N_3(0) \gtrless S(0)$, $P(0)$ to an arbitrary point $S(t)$, $P(t)$. Thus

$$\ln[P(t)/P(0)] = 3 \ln [S(t)/S(0)]$$

leads to $P(t) = P(0)[S(t)/S(0)]^3 \rightarrow P(0)[1/S(0)]^3$ as $t \rightarrow \infty$.

In other words, as $t \rightarrow \infty$, the solution lies on the hyperboloid

$$P = N_1 N_2 N_3 = P(0)[1/S(0)]^3 = C : C = \text{constant.}$$

But we also know that as $t \rightarrow \infty$, the solution lies in the inclined plane

$$S = N_1 + N_2 + N_3 = 1.$$

Combining these results leads to the conclusion that the solution asymptotically lies on the intersection of the hyperboloid with the inclined plane. This intersection is a closed curve whose size is determined by C, which in turn depends upon the initial conditions $N_1(0)$, $N_2(0)$, and $N_3(0)$. Solutions look like triangles with the vertices rounded.

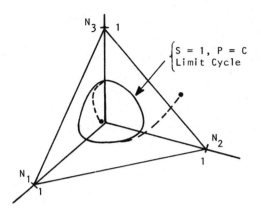

$$\begin{cases} S = 1, \ P = C \\ \text{Limit Cycle} \end{cases}$$

Before trying to make sense out of the solution to the above special case, let us look briefly at the general case $\alpha + \beta > 2$, with either $\alpha < 1$ or $\beta < 1$. Define

$$\gamma = \alpha + \beta - 2 > 0.$$

The equation for $S(t)$ then generalizes to

$$\frac{dS}{dt} = S(1 - S) + \gamma(N_1 N_2 + N_2 N_3 + N_3 N_1)$$

and the equation for $P(t)$ generalizes to

$$\frac{d \ln P}{dt} = -\gamma + (3 + \gamma)(1 - S).$$

Although we will not prove it, it turns out that as t gets large, the terms multiplying γ in the equation for S become small. The reason, as we will see, is that as t gets large, only one of N_1, N_2 and N_3 is more than vanishingly small at a time, thus all of the products $N_1 N_2$, . . . are small. The result is that as before,

$$S(t \to \infty) \to 1.$$

The equation for P then has the asymptotic solution

$$\ln\left[P(t)/P(0)\right] \rightarrow -\gamma t \text{ as } t \rightarrow \infty$$

thus

$$P(t) \rightarrow P(0) \exp\{-\gamma t\} \rightarrow 0.$$

Notice the nature of the solution is quite different than for the special case $\alpha + \beta = 2$. Specifically, although as before the solution lies in the inclined plane $S = 1$, now the product of the three populations, P, becomes asymptotically small, but never converges to any single point since there are no stable points if $\alpha + \beta > 2$ and either $\alpha > 0$ or $\beta > 0$.

Physically, what happens is this: as time passes, the state of the system approaches a situation with two species almost absent, and the third plentiful. This situation persists for a time; the state then shifts abruptly so that a different (determined by the equations) species is plentiful, and the other two almost vanish. This situation persists for a longer time than the previous one, but then shifts so that the third species becomes plentiful,. . .

Biologically these results are of course nonsense. The stable limit cycle only occurs for a situation of measure zero. The case with non-zero measure gives absurd results. Clearly, the idea of extinction has been neglected. Still, even given the physically unrealistic results, the exercise was informative. Specifically, our experience with two-species systems led us to expect stable points or stable limit cycles. The addition of a third competing species has added quite another possibility. Specifically, we have found a type of cycle which proceeds in an ever slower fashion. The explanation is related to the biologically reasonable non-transitive situation where in pairwise competition, 1 beats 2, 2 beats 3 and 3 beats 1. This is obviously not possible with just two species present.

1. The equations for two-species competition are given as:

$$\frac{dX}{dT} = rX(1 - \alpha_{11}X - \alpha_{12}Y)$$
$$\frac{dY}{dT} = rY(1 - \alpha_{21}X - \alpha_{22}Y)$$
$$r, \ \alpha\text{'s} > 0.$$

Show that it is possible to rewrite these equations in the form

$$\frac{dx}{dt} = x(1 - x - ay)$$
$$\frac{dy}{dt} = y(1 - bx - y)$$
$$a, b > 0$$

by making a suitable change of variables. (Note that nothing need be set equal to unity. Make the correspondence in your change of variables clear.)

2. Consider the pair of equations in problem 1 for $x(t)$ and $y(t)$. Assume that $a = b = 1$ and that $x(0) = 1.5$ and $y(0) = 0.5$. Use a method of solution analogous to the one used for three species competition to determine the possible asymptotic behavior of $x(t)$ and $y(t)$ as $t \to \infty$.

References

The material in this section of this monograph was drawn almost entirely from the one paper listed below:

May, R.M. and W.J. Leonard, "Nonlinear Aspects of Competition Between Three Species", SIAM Journal of Applied Mathematics, Volume 29, Number 2, pp. 243-253, September, 1975.

This is an interesting and readable account of the model for three species competition which forms the basis for this section of this monograph. Further references are cited in this paper.

11 Complexity vs. Stability

Biological Observation

A tropical rain forest is ecologically more stable than the sub-arctic tundra. If the number of species present is chosen as a measure of the 'complexity' of the ecosystem, and the ability of the species present to persist in time is taken as a sign of 'stability' then the above examples are interpreted to mean that Complexity leads to Stability. Another example of this hypothesis comes from agricultural observations. In general, a field with several interplanted crops is more resistant to a pest outbreak than a field with just a single crop.

Trophic Levels and Chains

Roughly speaking, trophic levels and chains are concerned with who eats whom. Animals at the same trophic level compete with one another for resources, while a predator is at a higher trophic level than its prey. We can employ this idea to construct a 'food web' such as the one shown below:

Large Carnivores

Small Carnivores

Herbivores

Vegetation

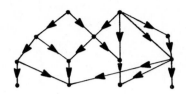

Note that the chain is not always neat for a real system, and it is sometimes a bit uncertain as to just which trophic level a particular species resides at.

Since we will not be able to simply write down a model to assess whether we agree that complexity leads to stability, we will instead proceed through a sequence of models that study a small piece of the bigger question.

Complexity at a single trophic level - n species competition

n = 2: We begin by reviewing our previous model for two-species competition. The food web shown to the left illustrates the case under study. Note that for future convenience, we give the parameters of the model different names than when we first considered the model.

$$\frac{dX_1}{dt} = X_1 \left[a_1 - \alpha_{11}X_1 - \alpha_{12}X_2 \right] \left.\begin{array}{c} \\ \\ \\ \\ \end{array}\right\} \quad a's, \alpha's > 0.$$

$$\frac{dX_2}{dt} = X_2 \left[a_2 - \alpha_{21}X_1 - \alpha_{22}X_2 \right]$$

Although we were able to study this model by linearized stability analysis, it is more transparent to consider instead our graphical method of solution.

Recall that the equilibrium with both species present occurs at the intersection of the two lines

$$\alpha_{11}X_1^* + \alpha_{12}X_2^* = a_1$$

$$\alpha_{12}X_1^* + \alpha_{22}X_2^* = a_2.$$

Further, if the equilibrium is to be stable, it is necessary that

$$\alpha_{11}\alpha_{22} - \alpha_{12}\alpha_{21} > 0.$$

n = 3: Using the same notation as above, the equations for three species competition are given by

$$\frac{dX_i}{dt} = X_i\left[a_i - \sum_{j=1}^{3} \alpha_{ij}X_j\right] : i = 1, 2, 3, \ a's, \alpha's > 0.$$

An equilibrium with all species present occurs if there is a unique solution to the equations:

$$\underset{\sim}{\alpha}\, \vec{X}* = \vec{a} : \underset{\sim}{\alpha} = (\alpha_{ij}),\ \vec{X}* = (X_i^*),\ \vec{a} = (a_i).$$

Notice that these are the equations for three planes in a three dimensional space. The planes must intersect in the first octant, and also must satisfy 2 inequalities (similar to the one above) if the equilibrium is to be stable.

n general: The general case follows logically from the above two cases. Specifically, the equilibrium, if it exists, occurs at the intersection of n hyperplanes in an n dimensional space. Stability then requires that (n - 1) inequalities be simultaneously satisfied.

Since the interaction parameters, the α's, are properties of the system of animals and not freely available, as the dimensionality of the system increases, it becomes less likely that all n hyperplanes will intersect at a single point. It also becomes less likely that the (n - 1) inequalities which lead to stability will be satisfied. Thus for n species competition, it appears that complexity does not lead to stability.

Complexity at several trophic levels - n species predator-prey

n = 2: We will choose as our paradigm the improved predator-prey equations in which the prey is subject to a resource limitation. Although we have not considered this case before, it follows easily from the Lotka-Volterra model.

$$\frac{dR}{dt} = R[a - cR - \alpha F]$$
$$\frac{dF}{dt} = F[-b + \beta R]$$

: all parameters positive.

The equilibrium with both species present occurs at

$$R^* = b/\beta$$
$$F^* = [a - cR^*]/\alpha.$$

Clearly, if this is to lie in the first quadrant,

$$(a/c) > (b/\beta).$$

The arrows and isoclines for this situation are shown in the sketch below.

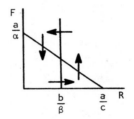

Note that the solution is always stable if the inequality which leads to equilibrium is satisfied.

The inequality has a rather simple interpretation. Notice from the original equation that if the predator species is absent ($F \equiv 0$), then

$$R^*\bigg|_{F\equiv0} = a/c = K_R \quad : \text{Carrying Capacity of R in the absence of F.}$$

On the other hand, if $F = F^*$

$$R^*\bigg|_{F=F^*} = b/\beta.$$

The inequality can then be seen to require that the Carrying Capacity of the prey be large enough to support the

-136-

predators when they are present.

n = 3:   The particular generalization that we will study is
shown in the diagram to the left. Note that there
is one species which is a prey only, one which is a
predator only, and one which is both. The generalization of the equations follows easily:

$$\frac{dR}{dt} = R\left[a - cR - \alpha_1 F_1\right]$$

$$\frac{dF_1}{dt} = F_1\left[-b_1 + \beta_1 R - \alpha_2 F_2\right]$$: all parameters positive.

$$\frac{dF_2}{dt} = F_2\left[-b_2 + \beta_2 F_1\right]$$

The equilibrium with all three species present occurs
at

$$F_1^* = b_2/\beta_2$$

$$R^* = (a - \alpha_1 F_1^*)/c$$

$$F_2^* = (\beta_1 R^* - b_1)/\alpha_2 .$$

We must also require that the point (R^*, F_1^*, F_2^*) lie in
the first octant. But notice that the restriction

$$R^* > b_1/\beta_1 > 0 \text{ means } F_2^* > 0 \text{ automatically,}$$

and, of course, $F_1^* > 0$ automatically also. Thus, as with
the two species analog, just one inequality must be satisfied to ensure that the three species equilibrium exists.
Further, as with the two species case, the equilibrium is
always stable if it exists.

The inequality can also be stated in the form

$$(a/c) > (b_1/\beta_1) + (\alpha_1 b_2/c\beta_2)$$

which admits the same interpretation as above. Specifically, the prey population in the absence of predation must
have a large enough Carrying Capacity to support the rest
of the species.

-137-

n general: For the linear chain with one species which acts
only as a prey, one which acts only as a predator, and (n - 2) which act as both, the results
follow directly as above. For any length chain
(though n much more than 4 is probably not realistic) only a single inequality need be satisfied.

We may therefore conclude that for this situation, the
more complex situation has the same stability as the simple
case.

The Lotka-Volterra Model extended - n predators and n prey

Note that this is a simpler sort of interaction than
the one described above, in that the prey do not exhibit
resource limitation. Recall that for the one predator one
prey case, the system exhibits neutrally stable cycles.
The interaction is shown schematically below

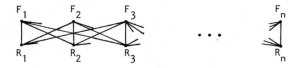

The mathematical model follows directly from the simple
Lotka-Volterra Equations:

$$\frac{dR_i}{dt} = R_i\left[a_i - \sum_{j=1}^{n} \alpha_{ij}F_j\right]$$

$$\frac{dF_i}{dt} = F_i\left[-b_i + \sum_{j=1}^{n} \beta_{ij}R_j\right]$$

$: i = 1,2,3,\ldots,n$
all parameters
non-negative.

Equilibrium: As usual, we are interested in the equilibrium point with all species present.

The equilibrium points are found by solving two (n x n)
sets of algebraic equations:

$$\sum_{j=1}^{n} \alpha_{ij} F_j^* = a_i$$

$$\sum_{j=1}^{n} \beta_{ij} R_j^* = b_i .$$

Note that in addition to being non-negative, the parameters must lead to $R_i^* > 0$ and $F_i^* > 0$.

Stability: Expand about (R_i^*, F_i^*), $R_i = R_i^*(1 + r_i)$, $F_i =$

$F_i^*(1 + f_i)$ to get

$$\frac{dr_i}{dt} = -\sum_{j=1}^{n} \alpha_{ij}^* f_j \quad : \alpha_{ij}^* = \alpha_{ij} F_j^*$$

$$\frac{df_i}{dt} = \sum_{j=1}^{n} \beta_{ij}^* r_j \quad : \beta_{ij}^* = \beta_{ij} R_j^* .$$

These equations can conveniently be represented in matrix form:

$$\begin{bmatrix} \frac{d\vec{r}}{dt} \\ \frac{d\vec{f}}{dt} \end{bmatrix} = \begin{bmatrix} 0 & | & -\alpha^* \\ - & - & - \\ +\beta^* & | & 0 \end{bmatrix} \begin{bmatrix} \vec{r} \\ \vec{f} \end{bmatrix} \quad \begin{cases} \vec{r} = (r_i) \\ \vec{f} = (f_i) \\ \alpha^* = (\alpha_{ij}^*) \\ \beta^* = (\beta_{ij}^*) \end{cases}$$

Assume: $\begin{bmatrix} \vec{r} \\ \vec{f} \end{bmatrix} = \begin{bmatrix} \vec{r}_0 \\ \vec{f}_0 \end{bmatrix} \exp\{\lambda t\} \rightarrow \det \begin{bmatrix} -I\lambda & | & -\alpha^* \\ - & - & - \\ +\beta^* & | & -I\lambda \end{bmatrix} = 0 .$

Characteristic Equation:

$$\lambda^{2n} + A_1 \lambda^{2(n-1)} + A_2 \lambda^{2(n-2)} + \cdots + A_{n-1} \lambda^2 + A_n = 0.$$

N.B. All of the odd powers are absent from the Characteristic Equation. It then follows simply that any poly-quadratic equation has roots of the form $\pm(x + iy)$. These are symmetric with respect to the origin in the complex λ plane.

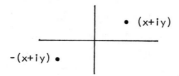

Based upon the structure of the roots in the complex plane, we can draw the following conclusions:

1. If all roots have $\text{Re}\{\lambda\} = 0$, we then have n pairs of purely imaginary conjugate roots. Like the one predator one prey Lotka-Volterra model, the stability is neutral.

2. If any root has $\text{Re}\{\lambda\} \neq 0$, then some root has $\text{Re}\{\lambda\} > 0$, thus the equilibrium with all species present is unstable.

We may therefore conclude that the n predator n prey Lotka-Volterra model is <u>at best</u> neutrally stable, and in general is less stable than the one predator one prey analog. Once again, we have found that for our models, complexity does not lead to stability.

Many species - Random interactions

Our next model will help to reconcile the apparent contradictions which we have found. Unfortunately, we will not be able to go through all of the mathematics. We will however report the result.

We consider a very general model for the interaction of n species:

$$\frac{dN_i}{dt} = F_i(N_1, N_2, N_3, \ldots, N_n) \ : \ i = 1, 2, 3, \ldots, n.$$

Equilibrium:

$$F_i(N_1^*, N_2^*, N_3^*, \ldots, N_n^*) = 0 \ : \ i = 1, 2, 3, \ldots, n.$$

N.B. The only restriction which we place on the functions $F_i(\cdot)$ is that they lead to an equilibrium solution

$(N_1^*, N_2^*, N_3^*, \ldots, N_n^*)$ with all species present.

Stability: Let $N_i = N_i^*(1 + x_i)$. Use Taylor Series to expand $F_i(\cdot)$ to get

$$N_i^* \frac{dx_i}{dt} = \sum_{j=1}^{n} \left. \frac{\partial F_i}{\partial N_j} \right|_{N_i = N_i^*} N_j^* x_j$$

which may be written

$$\frac{dx_i}{dt} = \sum_{j=1}^{n} \alpha_{ij} x_j \ : \ \alpha_{ij} = \frac{N_j^*}{N_i^*} \left. \frac{\partial F_i}{\partial N_j} \right|_{N_i = N_i^*}.$$

N.B. The matrix (α_{ij}) is often called the 'community matrix'.

We must now specify the structure of the 'community matrix'. We will do this in a random manner. We could conceive of doing this repeatedly, finding stability results for each, and then compiling the probability of a stable configuration.

1. Assume that each species is self-limiting, thus

$$\alpha_{jj} < 0.$$

N.B. By rescaling the x_j we may always choose $\alpha_{jj} = -1$.

2. Choose the α_{ij} ($i \neq j$) by doing the following two stage experiment.

    a. With Probability = 1 - C, set $\alpha_{ij} = 0$.

    b. With Probability = C, select α_{ij} from a distribution with mean = 0 and variance = S^2.

N.B. Think of C as the 'connectance' of the food web (the larger C, the more non-zero links), and think of S as a measure of the 'strength' of the interactions.

Since there will be roughly as many 'off diagonal' elements in the community matrix with plus as with minus signs, we expect to encounter competition, mutualism and predation.

<u>Asymptotic results for n >> 1</u>   (N.B. Calculation can actually be done by analytic methods, or else by repeated experimentation.)

It turns out that if

$S < 1/\sqrt{2nC}$: almost surely stable

$S > 1/\sqrt{2nC}$: almost surely unstable.

It is convenient and a bit surprising that the probability that the system is stable shifts rather abruptly at $S = 1/\sqrt{2nC}$.

Notice that if either C or S (or both) is large, we expect the system to be unstable. We therefore conclude that if a highly connected (complex) system with strong interactions is to be stable, it does not tend to have random interactions. This gives us a good clue to why field ecologists say that complexity leads to stability. Real ecosystems are assembled by nature in a manner which causes the unstable links to be lost and forgotten. Perhaps the proper way to state the initial hypothesis is that stability permits complexity (but not in a random manner.)

An alternative characterization of ecosystems has been proposed other than stability. The usual term employed is resilience. A one predator one prey model is clearly not resilient. If the prey should die out, the predator will also die out. On the other hand, if the food web contains many links, if one food species dies out, the species at higher trophic levels will simply substitute some other food into their diet, assuming such is available. This provides a functional definition of a resilient system. In population space, a resilient system will tend to respond to fluctuation by wandering around a little but will probably

not make any major excursion as a result of small pertur-
bations. A non-resilient system is like a house-of-cards.
Remove one element and the whole thing collapses.

References

The two references cited below provide a comprehensive
introduction to the profound questions which are touched
upon in the present section of this monograph.

May, R.M., Stability and Complexity in Model Ecosystems,
Princeton University Press, Princeton, N.J., 1973.

Much of the material presented in this section of this
monograph was drawn from Chapter 3 of this book. As
the title indicates, the central thrust of the entire
book is relevant to the topic under discussion.

Maynard Smith, J., Models in Ecology, Cambridge University
Press, Cambridge, 1974.

Chapters 7, 9, and 10 of this book discuss the questions of complexity and stability.

12 Solutions to Problems

12.1   Simple Single Species Population Models

1a. $\frac{dN}{dt} = R$, R constant, $N(0) \equiv N_0$.

1b. $\int_{N_0}^{N} d\tilde{N} = R \int_0^t d\tilde{t}$, $\rightarrow N(t) = N_0 + Rt$.

(This is of course the case of simple, linear growth.
It is unrealistic as a model for population growth in
virtually all cases.)

2. $\frac{dN}{dt} = r_0 N$, $r_0 > 0$, $N(0) \equiv N_0$.

Thus, $\int_{N_0}^{N} d \ln \tilde{N} = r_0 \int_0^t dt$, $\rightarrow \ln \frac{N(t)}{N_0} = r_0 t$.

Find $t = t^*$ such that $N(t^*) = 2N_0$, thus

$\ln \frac{2N_0}{N_0} = \ln 2 = r_0 t^* \Rightarrow t^* = \frac{\ln 2}{r_0} \doteq \frac{.693}{r_0}$.

(t* is the doubling time. If $r_0 = .025$, a value which
is not unrealistic for the current world human population, then $t^* \doteq 27.7$ years.)

3a. $\dfrac{dN}{dt} = \dfrac{r_0}{K}$ $(N-M)(K-N)$, $r_0, M, K > 0$, $M << K$.

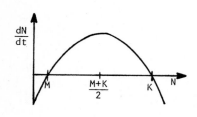

(Note: Curve is a parabola. Clearly,

$$\begin{cases} \dfrac{dN}{dt} < 0 \text{ for } N < M, \ N > K \\[2mm] \dfrac{dN}{dt} > 0 \text{ for } M < N < K \end{cases}$$

$M \equiv$ Minimum Viable Population

$K \equiv$ Carrying Capacity.)

3b. Equilibrium:

$$\dfrac{dN}{dt} = 0 \Rightarrow \dfrac{r_0}{K}(N-M)(K-N) = 0 \Rightarrow \begin{cases} N = M \\ N = K. \end{cases}$$

3c. Stability at $N = M$.

Let $N = M + x$. Then $\dfrac{dx}{dt} = r_0(1 - \dfrac{M}{K})x - \dfrac{r_0}{K}x^2$.

If $|x| << M << K$, or $|\dfrac{x^2}{K}| << |x|$, then we may linearize, to obtain $\dfrac{dx}{dt} = r_0(1 - \dfrac{M}{K})x$. Thus, $x(t) = x_0 e^{r_0(1 - \frac{M}{K})t}$ where x_0 is the small initial disturbance. Since $r_0 > 0$, $M << K \Rightarrow$ solution diverges from $x = 0$ as $t \to \infty$, thus $N = M$ is unstable.

Stability at $N = K$.

Let $N = K + y$. Then $\dfrac{dy}{dt} = -r_0(1 - \dfrac{M}{K})y - \dfrac{r_0}{K}y^2$.

If $|y| << K$, or $|\dfrac{y^2}{K}| << |y|$, then we may linearize, to obtain $\dfrac{dy}{dt} = -r_0(1 - \dfrac{M}{K})y$. Thus $y(t) = y_0 e^{-r_0(1 - \frac{M}{K})t}$ where y_0 is the small initial disturbance. Since $r_0 > 0$, $M << K \Rightarrow$ solution converges to $y = 0$ as $t \to \infty$, thus $N = K$ is stable. (A graphical stability analysis of figure in part a leads to conclusions that populations with $0 < N < M$ die out, while populations with

N > M converge to N = K. This is consistent with results of stability analysis.)

3d. Population Rate of Growth $\equiv \frac{dN}{dt}$.

Maximize: $\frac{d}{dN}\left(\frac{dN}{dt}\right) = 0 \Rightarrow \frac{r_0}{K}\left[(K - N) - (N - M)\right] = 0$

$$\Rightarrow K - 2N + M = 0, \rightarrow N = \frac{M + K}{2}.$$

3e. $\frac{dN}{dt} = \frac{r_0}{K}\left[(N - M)(K - N)\right]$, $N(0) \equiv N_0$. Separate and
integrate

$$\int_{N_0}^{N} \frac{d\tilde{N}}{(\tilde{N} - M)(\tilde{N} - K)} = -\frac{r_0}{K} \int_{0}^{t} dt.$$

Do integral on L.H.S. by partial fractions,

$$\frac{1}{(N - M)(N - K)} \equiv \frac{A}{N - M} + \frac{B}{N - K} = \frac{A(N - K) + B(N - M)}{(N - M)(N - K)}$$

$$\Rightarrow \left.\begin{array}{l} A + B = 0 \\[6pt] AK + BM = 1 \end{array}\right\} \Rightarrow A = \frac{-1}{K - M}, \ B = \frac{1}{K - M}$$

thus

$$-\frac{1}{K - M} \int_{N_0}^{N} \frac{d\tilde{N}}{\tilde{N} - M} + \frac{1}{K - M} \int_{N_0}^{N} \frac{d\tilde{N}}{\tilde{N} - K} = -\frac{r_0}{K} \int_{0}^{t} d\tilde{t},$$

$$\left[-\ell n \ (\tilde{N} - M) + \ell n \ (\tilde{N} - K)\right]_{N_0}^{N} = -r_0 (1 - \frac{M}{K})t,$$

$$\ell n \left[\frac{(N - K)(N_0 - M)}{(N_0 - K)(N - M)}\right] = -r_0 (1 - \frac{M}{K})t,$$

and, finally,

$$N(t) = \frac{K + M(\frac{K - N_0}{N_0 - M}) \ e^{-r_0 (1 - \frac{M}{K})t}}{1 + (\frac{K - N_0}{N_0 - M}) \ e^{-r_0 (1 - \frac{M}{K})t}}.$$

4a. $\frac{dN}{dt} = 1 - e^{-r_0(1 - \frac{N}{K})}$

   Equilibrium: $\frac{dN}{dt} = 0 \Rightarrow e^{-r_0(1 - \frac{N}{K})} = 1$

   $\Rightarrow -r_0(1 - \frac{N}{K}) = 0 \Rightarrow N = K.$

4b. Stability: Let $N = K + x$. This leads to

   $\frac{dx}{dt} = 1 - e^{\frac{r_0 x}{K}}.$

   Expand $e^{\frac{r_0 x}{K}}$ at $x = 0$, to obtain

   $e^{\frac{r_0 x}{K}} = 1 + \frac{r_0}{K}x + (\frac{r_0}{K})^2 x^2 + \cdots.$

   Thus

   $\frac{dx}{dt} = 1 - \left\{1 + \frac{r_0}{K}x + (\frac{r_0}{K})^2 x^2 + \cdots\right\} = -\frac{r_0}{K}x - (\frac{r_0}{K})^2 x^2 + \cdots.$

   if $|x| \ll K$, so that $\left|\frac{x^2}{K^2}\right| \ll \left|\frac{x}{K}\right|$, we may linearize and

   obtain

   $\frac{dx}{dt} = -\frac{r_0}{K}x, \rightarrow x(t) = x_0 e^{\frac{-r_0 t}{K}}$, where x_0 is the initial

   small disturbance.

   Since r_0 and K are positive, $x \rightarrow 0$ as $t \rightarrow \infty$, $\Rightarrow$ stable.

12.2   Stochastic Birth and Death Processes

1.   Solve: $\dfrac{dp_{j+2}(t)}{dt} + \lambda(j+2)\,p_{j+2}(t)$

$$= \lambda(j+1)j\,e^{-\lambda j t}\,(1 - e^{-\lambda t}) : p_{j+2}(0) = 0.$$

Multiply both sides by integrating factor $e^{\lambda(j+2)t}$ and integrate:

$$\int d\left\{e^{\lambda(j+2)t}\,p_{j+2}(t)\right\} = \lambda(j+1)j \int \left[e^{2\lambda t} - e^{\lambda t}\right]dt$$

$$e^{\lambda(j+2)t}\,p_{j+2}(t) = \lambda(j+1)j\left[\frac{e^{2\lambda t}}{2\lambda} - \frac{e^{\lambda t}}{\lambda}\right] + C.$$

Use $p_{j+2}(0) = 0$ to evaluate C:

$$C = -\lambda(j+1)j\left[\frac{1}{2\lambda} - \frac{1}{\lambda}\right] = \frac{(j+1)j}{2}.$$

Thus

$$p_{j+2}(t) = e^{-\lambda(j+2)t}\left\{\frac{(j+1)j}{2}\left[e^{2\lambda t} - 2e^{\lambda t} + 1\right]\right\}$$

$$= \frac{(j+1)j}{2}\,e^{-\lambda j t}\left[1 - e^{-\lambda t}\right]^2.$$

2.   Given:
$$p_{k-1}(t) = \binom{k-2}{j-1}e^{-\lambda j t}\left[1 - e^{-\lambda t}\right]^{k-j-1}$$

Find $p_k(t)$ by induction using D - ΔE:

$$\frac{dp_k(t)}{dt} + \lambda k\,p_k(t) = \lambda(k-1)\,p_{k-1}(t)$$

$$= \lambda(k-1)\binom{k-2}{j-1}e^{-\lambda j t}\left[1 - e^{-\lambda t}\right]^{k-j-1}.$$

Multiply both sides by integrating factor $e^{\lambda k t}$ and integrate:

$$\int d\left\{e^{\lambda k t}\,p_k(t)\right\} = \lambda(k-1)\binom{k-2}{j-1}\int e^{\lambda(k-j)t}\left[1 - e^{-\lambda t}\right]^{k-j-1}dt$$

$$e^{\lambda k t}\, p_k(t) = \binom{k-1}{j-1}(k-j)\int \left[e^{\lambda t} - 1\right]^{k-j-1} \lambda e^{\lambda t}\, dt$$

$$= \binom{k-1}{j-1}(k-j)\left\{\frac{\left[e^{\lambda t} - 1\right]^{k-j}}{k-j}\right\} + C.$$

But $p_k(0) = 0$ for $k > j \Rightarrow C = 0$, thus

$$p_k(t) = \binom{k-1}{j-1} e^{-\lambda k t} \left[e^{\lambda t} - 1\right]^{k-j}$$

$$= \binom{k-1}{j-1} e^{-\lambda j t} \left[1 - e^{-\lambda t}\right]^{k-j} \qquad \text{QED.}$$

3a. $\displaystyle E(N) = \sum_{i=j}^{\infty} i\, p_i(t) = \sum_{i=j}^{\infty} i\binom{i-1}{j-1} e^{-\lambda j t} \left[1 - e^{-\lambda t}\right]^{i-j}$

$$= e^{-\lambda j t} \sum_{k=0}^{\infty} (j+k) \binom{j+k-1}{j-1} \left[1 - e^{-\lambda t}\right]^{k}$$

$$= j e^{-\lambda j t} \sum_{k=0}^{\infty} \binom{j+k}{j} \left[1 - e^{-\lambda t}\right]^{k},$$

But recall that $\displaystyle (1 - x)^{-(s+1)} = \sum_{r=0}^{\infty} \binom{s+r}{s} x^{r}$,
thus

$$E(N) = j e^{-\lambda j t} \left\{1 - \left[1 - e^{-\lambda t}\right]\right\}^{-(j+1)}$$

$$= j e^{-\lambda j t}\, e^{\lambda(j+1)t} = j e^{\lambda t}.$$

$\displaystyle E(N^2) = \sum_{i=j}^{\infty} i^2\, p_i(t) = \sum_{i=j}^{\infty} i^2 \binom{i-1}{j-1} e^{-\lambda j t} \left[1 - e^{-\lambda t}\right]^{i-j}$

$$= e^{-\lambda j t} \sum_{k=0}^{\infty} (j+k)^2 \binom{j+k-1}{j-1} \left[1 - e^{-\lambda t}\right]^{k}$$

$$= j e^{-\lambda j t} \sum_{k=0}^{\infty} (j+k) \binom{j+k}{j} \left[1 - e^{-\lambda t}\right]^{k}$$

$$= j(j+1) e^{-\lambda j t} \sum_{k=0}^{\infty} \binom{j+k+1}{j+1} \left[1 - e^{-\lambda t}\right]^{k}$$

$$- j e^{-\lambda j t} \sum_{k=0}^{\infty} \binom{j+k}{j} \left[1 - e^{-\lambda t}\right]^{k}.$$

- 150-

As above,

$$= j(j+1)e^{-\lambda j t} \, e^{\lambda(j+2)t} - je^{-\lambda j t} \, e^{\lambda(j+1)t}.$$

Thus

$$E(N^2) = j(j+1) \, e^{2\lambda t} - je^{\lambda t}$$

and

$$V(N) = E(N^2) - E(N)^2 = j(j+1)e^{2\lambda t} - je^{\lambda t} - j^2 e^{2\lambda t}$$

$$= je^{2\lambda t} - je^{\lambda t} = je^{\lambda t} \left[e^{\lambda t} - 1 \right].$$

3b. Given: $\dfrac{dp_i(t)}{dt} = -\lambda i \, p_i(t) + \lambda(i - 1) \, p_{i-1}(t),$

$$E(N) = \sum_{i=j}^{\infty} i \, p_i(t)$$

$$\frac{dE(N)}{dt} = \sum_{i=j}^{\infty} i \frac{dp_i(t)}{dt} = \sum_{i=j}^{\infty} \left[-\lambda i^2 \, p_i(t) \right.$$

$$\left. + \lambda i (i-1) \, p_{i-1}(t) \right]$$

$$= \lambda \sum_{k=j}^{\infty} p_k(t) \left[k(k+1) - k^2 \right] = \lambda \sum_{k=j}^{\infty} kp_k(t) = \lambda E(N).$$

Thus, solve

$$\frac{dE(N)}{dt} = \lambda E(N) \; : \; E(N) = j \text{ at } t = 0$$

to get

$$E(N) = je^{\lambda t}.$$

$$E(N^2) = \sum_{i=j}^{\infty} i^2 \, p_i(t)$$

$$\frac{dE(N^2)}{dt} = \sum_{i=j}^{\infty} i^2 \frac{dp_i(t)}{dt} = \sum_{i=j}^{\infty} \left[-\lambda i^3 \, p_i(t) \right.$$

$$\left. + \lambda i^2 (i-1) \, p_{i-1}(t) \right]$$

$$= \lambda \sum_{k=j}^{\infty} p_k(t) \left[(k+1)^2 \, k - k^3 \right]$$

$$= \lambda \sum_{k=j}^{\infty} p_k(t) \left[2k^2 + k \right]$$

$$= 2\lambda \, E(N^2) + \lambda E(N).$$

Thus, solve

$$\frac{dE(N^2)}{dt} - 2\lambda \, E(N^2) = j\lambda e^{\lambda t}.$$

Multiply by integrating factor $e^{-2\lambda t}$ and integrate:

$$\int d\left\{ e^{-2\lambda t} \, E(N^2) \right\} = j\lambda \int e^{-\lambda t} \, dt,$$

thus

$$e^{-2\lambda t} \, E(N^2) = -je^{-\lambda t} + C.$$

Since $V(N) = 0$ at $t = 0 \Rightarrow E(N^2) = E(N)^2 = j^2$ at $t = 0$.

Use this to find C:

$$j^2 = -j + C \rightarrow C = j^2 + j.$$

Hence

$$E(N^2) = (j^2 + j)e^{2\lambda t} - je^{\lambda t}$$

and

$$V(N) = E(N^2) - E(N)^2 = (j^2 + j)e^{2\lambda t} - je^{\lambda t} - j^2 e^{2\lambda t}$$
$$= je^{2\lambda t} - je^{\lambda t} = je^{\lambda t}\left[e^{\lambda t} - 1 \right].$$

4. As in # 3b,

$$\frac{dE(N^2)}{dt} = \sum_{i=1}^{\infty} i^2 \frac{dp_i(t)}{dt} = \sum_{i=1}^{\infty} \left[-(\lambda + \mu)i^3 \, p_i(t) \right.$$
$$+ \lambda i^2 (i - 1)p_{i-1}(t)$$
$$\left. + \mu i^2 (i + 1) \, p_{i+1}(t) \right]$$

$$= \lambda \sum_{i=1}^{\infty} \left[-i^3 p_i + i^2 (i - 1)p_{i-1} \right]$$

$$+ \mu \sum_{i=1}^{\infty} \left[-i^3 p_i + i^2 (i + 1)p_{i+1} \right]$$

$$= \lambda \sum_{k=0}^{\infty} p_k \left[(k + 1)^2 k - k^3 \right]$$

$$+ \mu \sum_{k=0}^{\infty} p_k \left[(k - 1)^2 k - k^3 \right]$$

$$= \lambda \sum_{k=0}^{\infty} p_k \left[2k^2 + k\right] + \mu \sum_{k=0}^{\infty} p_k \left[-2k^2 + k\right]$$

$$= 2(\lambda - \mu) \sum_{k=0}^{\infty} k^2 p_k + (\lambda + \mu) \sum_{k=0}^{\infty} k p_k$$

$$= 2(\lambda - \mu) E(N^2) + (\lambda + \mu) E(N).$$

Thus, we must solve

$$\frac{dE(N^2)}{dt} + 2(\mu - \lambda)E(N^2) = (\lambda + \mu)j e^{(\lambda-\mu)t}.$$

Multiply through by integrating factor $e^{2(\mu-\lambda)t}$ and integrate

to get

$$e^{2(\mu-\lambda)t} E(N^2) = (\lambda + \mu)j \int e^{(\mu-\lambda)t} \, dt$$

$$= -j \frac{\lambda+\mu}{\lambda-\mu} e^{(\mu-\lambda)t} + C.$$

Use $V(N) = 0$ at $t = 0$ to evaluate C

to get

$$E(N^2) = E(N)^2 = j^2 \text{ at } t = 0.$$

Thus

$$j^2 = -j \frac{\lambda+\mu}{\lambda-\mu} + C \rightarrow C = j^2 + j \frac{\lambda+\mu}{\lambda-\mu}.$$

Hence

$$E(N^2) = -j \frac{\lambda+\mu}{\lambda-\mu} e^{(\lambda-\mu)t} + \left[j^2 + j \frac{\lambda+\mu}{\lambda-\mu}\right] e^{2(\lambda-\mu)t}$$

and

$$V(N) = E(N^2) - E(N)^2$$

$$= j \frac{\lambda+\mu}{\lambda-\mu} \left[e^{2(\lambda-\mu)t} - e^{(\lambda-\mu)t}\right] + j^2 e^{2(\lambda-\mu t)}$$

$$- j^2 e^{2(\lambda-\mu)t}$$

$$V(N) = j \frac{\lambda+\mu}{\lambda-\mu} e^{(\lambda-\mu)t} \left[e^{(\lambda-\mu)t} - 1\right].$$

5. $E(N) = je^{(\lambda-\mu)t}$.

If $\lambda = \mu \Rightarrow E(N) = j$

$V(N) = j\,\dfrac{\lambda+\mu}{\lambda-\mu}\,e^{(\lambda-\mu)t}\left[e^{(\lambda-\mu)t} - 1\right]$

If $\lambda = \mu \Rightarrow V(N) = \dfrac{0}{0}$ (Indeterminate form)

Let $\rho \equiv \lambda - \mu \Rightarrow \lambda\rho = \rho + \mu,\ \lambda + \mu = \rho + 2\mu$

$\rightarrow V\rho(N) = j\,\dfrac{2\mu+\rho}{\rho}\,e^{\rho t}\left[e^{\rho t} - 1\right] = j\,\dfrac{2\mu+\rho}{\rho}\left[e^{2\rho t} - e^{\rho t}\right]$

$\displaystyle\lim_{\rho \to 0} V_\rho(N) = 2j\mu\,\dfrac{1-1}{0} = \dfrac{0}{0}$

Apply l'Hopital's Rule $\rightarrow$

$\displaystyle\lim_{\rho \to 0} V_\rho(N) = \lim_{\rho \to 0} \dfrac{j(2\mu+\rho)\left[2te^{2\rho t} - te^{\rho t}\right] + j\left[e^{2\rho t} - e^{\rho t}\right]}{1}$

$\rightarrow j(2\mu)\left[2t - t\right] = 2j\mu t$.

Thus if $\lambda = \mu \leftrightarrows \rho = 0 \Rightarrow E(N) = j$ (constant)

$\qquad\qquad\qquad\qquad\qquad V(N) = 2j\mu t$ (grows linearly
$\qquad\qquad\qquad\qquad\qquad\qquad\qquad\qquad\qquad$ with time)

12.3　Two Age Group Population Model

1. $\dfrac{N(t + \Delta t) - N(t)}{\Delta t} = r_0 N(t)$: $N(0) = N_0$

    a)　$\rightarrow N(t + \Delta t) = (1 + r_0 \Delta t) N(t)$

        thus with $t = 0$: $N(\Delta t) = (1 + r_0 \Delta t) N_0$

            with $t = \Delta t$: $N(2\Delta t) = (1 + r_0 \Delta t) N(\Delta t)$

$$= (1 + r_0 \Delta t)^2 N_0$$

$$\vdots$$

        and with $t = (k-1)\Delta t$: $N(k\Delta t) = (1 + r_0 \Delta t) N\left[(k-1)\Delta t\right]$

$$= (1 + r_0 \Delta t)^k N_0 .$$

    b)　$\displaystyle\lim_{\Delta t \to 0} \dfrac{N(t + \Delta t) - N(t)}{\Delta t} = \dfrac{dN(t)}{dt} = r_0 N(t)$: $N(0) = N_0$

$$\rightarrow \int_{N_0}^{N(t)} \dfrac{d\tilde{N}}{\tilde{N}} = r_0 \int_0^t d\tilde{t} \rightarrow N(t) = N_0 e^{r_0 t} .$$

    c)　$N(k\Delta t) = N_0 (1 + r_0 \Delta t)^k$

        To take limit, let $k\Delta t \rightarrow t \Rightarrow \Delta t = \dfrac{t}{k}$ as $\begin{smallmatrix} k\to\infty \\ \Delta t \to 0 \end{smallmatrix}$

        Thus $N(t) = \displaystyle\lim_{k\to\infty} N_0 (1 + \dfrac{r_0 t}{k})^k \rightarrow N_0 e^{r_0 t}$

        $\Rightarrow \displaystyle\lim_{k\to\infty} (1 + \dfrac{x}{k})^k = e^x$

        $e^x = 1 + x + \dfrac{x^2}{2!} + \dfrac{x^3}{3!} + \cdots$

> N.B. This implies that it does not matter when you let $\Delta t \to 0$. Same result whether done in Δ.E. $\rightarrow$ D.E. or in solution.

        $(1 + \dfrac{x}{k})^k = \displaystyle\sum_{j=0}^{k} \binom{k}{j} (\dfrac{x}{k})^j = 1 + k(\dfrac{x}{k}) + \dfrac{(k)(k-1)}{2!} (\dfrac{x}{k})^2$

$$+ \dfrac{(k)(k-1)(k-2)}{3!} (\dfrac{x}{k})^3$$

$$+ \cdots$$

        $\displaystyle\lim_{k\to\infty} (1 + \dfrac{x}{k})^k = 1 + x + \dfrac{x^2}{2!} + \dfrac{x^3}{3!} + \cdots = e^x$　Q.E.D.

2. $\dfrac{N(t + \Delta t) - N(t)}{\Delta t} = r_0 N(t) \left[1 - \dfrac{N(t)}{K}\right]$

   Let $\Delta t = 1$

   $N(t + 1) = (1 + r_0)N(t) - \dfrac{r_0}{K}N^2(t)$

   Next, let $N(t) = B_{t-1} \leftrightharpoons N(t + 1) = B_t$

   and $(1 + r_0) = R_0 \to r_0 = (R_0 - 1)$

   $\to B_t = R_0 B_{t-1} - \dfrac{(R_0 - 1)}{K} B_{t-1}^2$

   Finally, let $\dfrac{(R_0 - 1)}{K} = \dfrac{R_0 \ell_0}{H} \Rightarrow K = H\dfrac{(R_0 - 1)}{R_0 \ell_0} = B_e$

   $\to B_t = R_0 B_{t-1} - \dfrac{R_0 \ell_0}{H} B_{t-1}^2.$

N.B. Since this equation is identical to discrete time logistic and its solution is very different than continuous time logistic, letting $\Delta t \to 0$ has had a profound effect upon results.

3. Given: $\left. \begin{array}{l} B_t = m_0 A_t \left[1 - \dfrac{A_t}{H}\right] \\[2mm] A_t = \ell_0 B_{t-1} \end{array} \right\} R_0 = \ell_0 m_0.$

   Equilibrium: Let $B_t = B_{t-1} = B_e \Rightarrow A_e = \ell_0 B_e$

   and $B_e = \underbrace{m_0 \ell_0}_{R_0} B_e \left[1 - \dfrac{A_e}{H}\right] \Rightarrow A_e = H(1 - \dfrac{1}{R_0}) = H\dfrac{(R_0 - 1)}{R_0}$

   and $B_e = H\dfrac{(R_0 - 1)}{R_0 \ell_0}$.

   Next, linearize equations -

   Let $\left. \begin{array}{l} B_t = B_e + b_t \\[2mm] A_t = A_e + a_t \end{array} \right\}$ where $\left|\dfrac{b_t}{B_e}\right|, \left|\dfrac{a_t}{A_e}\right| \ll 1.$

   1st equation:

   $B_t = m_0 A_t \left[1 - \dfrac{A_t}{H}\right] \to B_e + b_t = m_0(A_e + a_t)\left[1 - \dfrac{A_e + a_t}{H}\right]$

-156-

thus

$$B_e + b_t = m_0(\ell_0 B_e + a_t) \left[1 - (1 - \frac{1}{R_0}) - \frac{a_t}{H}\right]$$

$$= (R_0 B_e + m_0 a_t)\left[\frac{1}{R_0} - \frac{a_t}{H}\right]$$

$$= B_e + \left[\frac{m_0}{R_0} - \frac{R_0 B_e}{H}\right] a_t - \frac{m_0}{H} a_t^2$$

hence

$$b_t = \frac{1}{\ell_0} \left[1 - (R_0 - 1)\right] a_t - \frac{m_0}{H} a_t^2$$

Linearize $\Leftarrow$ ignore a_t^2 terms $\rightarrow$

$$b_t = \frac{1}{\ell_0} \left[2 - R_0\right] a_t .$$

2nd equation:

$$A_t = \ell_0 B_{t-1} \rightarrow A_e + a_t = \ell_0 \left[B_e + b_{t-1}\right]$$

$$\rightarrow a_t = \ell_0 b_{t-1} .$$

Thus linearized equations are

$$b_t = \frac{1}{\ell_0}\left[2 - R_0\right] a_t \text{ and } a_t = \ell_0 b_{t-1} .$$

Observe: If $R_0 = 1$, 1st equation is $b_t = \frac{1}{\ell_0} a_t$

$R_0 = 2$, 1st equation is $b_t = 0$

$R_0 = 3$, 1st equation is $b_t = -\frac{1}{\ell_0} a_t .$

Hence

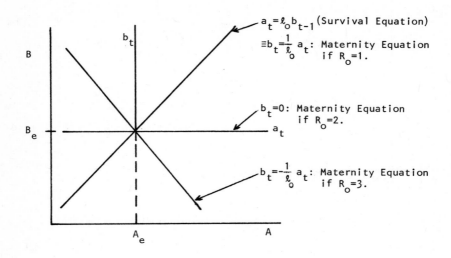

$a_t = \ell_o b_{t-1}$ (Survival Equation)

$\equiv b_t = \frac{1}{\ell_o} a_t$: Maternity Equation if $R_o = 1$.

$b_t = 0$: Maternity Equation if $R_o = 2$.

$b_t = -\frac{1}{\ell_o} a_t$: Maternity Equation if $R_o = 3$.

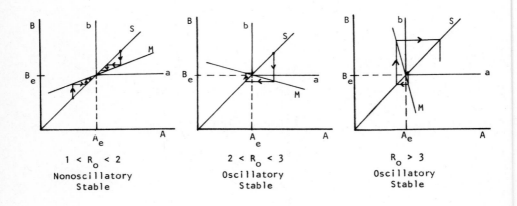

$1 < R_o < 2$
Nonoscillatory
Stable

$2 < R_o < 3$
Oscillatory
Stable

$R_o > 3$
Oscillatory
Stable

N.B.   Linearized analysis extends local behavior near
       (B_e, A_e) outward to infinity - did not happen with
       non-linear analysis.

-158-

12.4 Time Delayed Logistic Equations

1a. $Q(\zeta) = \dfrac{\zeta}{T^2} e^{-\frac{\zeta}{T}}$

$\dfrac{dQ}{d\zeta} = \dfrac{1}{T^2} \left(1 - \dfrac{\zeta}{T}\right) e^{-\frac{\zeta}{T}} = 0 \Rightarrow \zeta = T$

$\dfrac{d^2Q}{d\zeta^2} = \dfrac{1}{T^2} \left[\left(1 - \dfrac{\zeta}{T}\right)\left(-\dfrac{1}{T}\right) - \dfrac{1}{T} \right] e^{-\frac{\zeta}{T}}$

$\dfrac{d^2Q}{d\zeta^2} \bigg|_{\zeta=T} = \dfrac{-1}{T^3} e^{-1} < 0 \text{ for } T > 0 \Rightarrow \text{maximum.}$

1b. $\hat{Q}(\lambda) \equiv \displaystyle\int_0^\infty e^{-\lambda\zeta} Q(\zeta) d\zeta$

$= \dfrac{1}{T^2} \displaystyle\int_0^\infty \zeta \, e^{-(\lambda + \frac{1}{T})\zeta} \, d\zeta : \quad \begin{array}{l} u = \zeta, \quad dv = e^{-(\lambda + \frac{1}{T})\zeta} d\zeta \\[2mm] du = d\zeta, \quad v = -\dfrac{e^{-(\lambda + \frac{1}{T})\zeta}}{(\lambda + \frac{1}{T})} \end{array}$

$= \dfrac{1}{T^2} \left\{ \dfrac{-\zeta e^{-(\lambda + \frac{1}{T})\zeta}}{(\lambda + \frac{1}{T})} \bigg|_0^\infty + \dfrac{1}{\lambda + \frac{1}{T}} \displaystyle\int_0^\infty e^{-(\lambda + \frac{1}{T})\zeta} d\zeta \right\}$

$= \dfrac{1}{T^2} \left(\dfrac{1}{\lambda + \frac{1}{T}}\right)^2 \underbrace{\left[-e^{-(\lambda + \frac{1}{T})\zeta}\right]_o^\infty}_{= 1} = \dfrac{1}{(1+\lambda T)^2} \, .$

2. $P(\lambda) = \lambda^3 + a\lambda^2 + b\lambda + c = 0$

Routh array

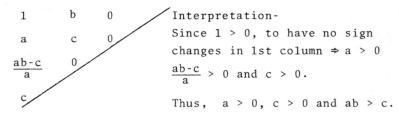

1	b	0
a	c	0
$\dfrac{ab-c}{a}$	0	
c		

Interpretation-
Since $1 > 0$, to have no sign changes in 1st column $\Rightarrow a > 0$

$\dfrac{ab-c}{a} > 0$ and $c > 0$.

Thus, $a > 0$, $c > 0$ and $ab > c$.

3. $P(\lambda) = \lambda^5 - 3\lambda^4 - 23\lambda^3 - 33\lambda^2 + 166\lambda + 120 = 0$

Routh array

$$
\begin{array}{cccc}
1 & -23 & 166 & 0 \\
-3 & -33 & 120 & \\
-34 & 206 & 0 & \\
\dfrac{-870}{17} & 120 & & \\
\dfrac{10986}{87} & 0 & & \\
120 & & &
\end{array}
$$

$$\begin{vmatrix} 1 & -23 \\ -3 & -33 \end{vmatrix} \Big/ {+3} = \frac{-33-69}{3} = -34$$

$$\begin{vmatrix} 1 & 166 \\ -3 & 120 \end{vmatrix} \Big/ {+3} = \frac{120+498}{3} = 206$$

$$\begin{vmatrix} -3 & -33 \\ -34 & 206 \end{vmatrix} \Big/ {+34} = \frac{-618-1122}{34} = -\frac{870}{17}$$

$$\begin{vmatrix} -34 & 206 \\ \dfrac{-870}{17} & 120 \end{vmatrix} \Big/ \dfrac{870}{17} = \frac{-4080+\dfrac{179220}{17}}{\dfrac{870}{17}} = \frac{10986}{87} \; .$$

2 sign changes $\leftrightarrows$ 2 roots in RHP.

N.B. $P(\lambda) = 0$ has roots $\lambda = -1, -2, -3, 4, 5$.

4. $\dfrac{N(t + \Delta t) - N(t)}{\Delta t} = r(N)\, N(t) : r(N) = r_0 \left[1 - \dfrac{N(t - \Delta t)}{K} \right].$

a) $\Delta t = T \rightarrow N(t + T) - N(t) = r_0 T\, N(t) \left[1 - \dfrac{N(t - T)}{K} \right].$

Equilibrium: $N(t + T) = N(t) = N(t - T) \equiv N_e \Rightarrow$

$$0 = (r_0 T) N_e \left[1 - \frac{N_e}{K} \right] \Rightarrow N_e = K.$$

Stability: Let $N(z) = K[1 + x(z)] : z = t \pm jT,\ j = 0, 1, 2$

$\rightarrow$

$K[x(t + T) - x(t)] = K r_0 T [1 + x(t)] [- x(t - T)]$

$x(t + T) - x(t) = -r_0 T x(t-T) - r_0 T\, x(t) x(t-T).$

Linearize: $|x| \ll 1 \Rightarrow |x^2| \ll |x|$ thus

$x(t + T) - x(t) = -r_0 T\, x(t - T).$

Assume solution is of same form as always, that is,

$x(z) = A \Lambda^z : z = t \pm jT,\ j = 0, 1, 2, \ldots$

A, Λ constants.

-160-

Thus:

$$A\Lambda^{t+T} - A\Lambda^t = -r_0 T A \Lambda^{t-T}$$

$\rightarrow$

$$\underbrace{A\Lambda^{t-T}}_{\neq 0} \quad \underbrace{\left[\Lambda^{2T} - \Lambda^T + r_0 T\right]}_{= 0} = 0$$

$\neq 0 \quad \Rightarrow \qquad = 0$: Characteristic Equation.

Solve C.E. using quadratic formula:

$$\Lambda^T_{\frac{1}{2}} = \frac{1 \pm \sqrt{1 - 4r_0 T}}{2}$$

Thus

$$x(t) = A_1\left[\frac{1}{2} + \frac{1}{2}\sqrt{1 - 4r_0 T}\right]^{t/T} + A_2\left[\frac{1}{2} - \frac{1}{2}\sqrt{1 - 4r_0 T}\right]^{t/T}$$

Where A_1 and A_2 depend upon the initial distur-bance from equilibrium, x_0.

Character of $x(t)$:

Clearly, if $|\Lambda^T_1| < 1$ and $|\Lambda^T_2| < 1$, $x(t) \rightarrow 0$ as $t \rightarrow \infty$.

Roots purely real if $1 - 4r_0 T > 0 \Rightarrow r_0 T < \frac{1}{4}$

(on physical grounds, $r_0 T > 0$)

and when $r_0 T = \frac{1}{4}$, $\Lambda^T_1 = \Lambda^T_2 = (\frac{1}{2})$

If $r_0 T > \frac{1}{4}$, $\Lambda^T_{\frac{1}{2}} = \left[\frac{1}{2} \pm \frac{1}{2} i\sqrt{4r_0 T - 1}\right]$: $i = \sqrt{-1}$

and $|\Lambda^T_{\frac{1}{2}}| = 1 \leqslant (\frac{1}{2})^2 + (\frac{1}{2}\sqrt{4r_0 T - 1})^2 = 1$

$$\Rightarrow \frac{1}{4} + r_0 T - \frac{1}{4} = r_0 T = 1$$

$\Rightarrow$ solution is stable if $0 < r_0 T < 1$
and unstable if $r_0 T > 1$

(N.B. $r_0 T = \frac{1}{4}$ is transition from non-oscillatory to oscillatory point.)

b)

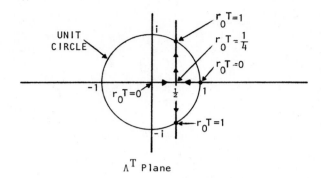

Λ^T Plane

Roots: $r_0 T = 0$, at 0, 1

$r_0 T = \frac{1}{4}$, at $\frac{1}{2}$, $\frac{1}{2}$

$r_0 T = 1$, at $\frac{1}{2} + i\frac{\sqrt{3}}{2}$, $\frac{1}{2} - i\frac{\sqrt{3}}{2}$.

Note: Stable $\leftrightarrows$ roots inside unit circle. Unstable $\leftrightarrows$ roots outside unit circle. (Nonoscillatory roots on positive real axis.)

c)   We have studied four very similar cases - two with time treated as a continuous variable, two with time treated as a discrete variable. These are:

I: $\dfrac{dN(t)}{dt} = r_0 N(t)\left[1 - \dfrac{1}{K}\displaystyle\int_{-\infty}^{t} N(\tau)Q(t-\tau)d\tau\right]$

$Q(z) = \dfrac{z}{T^2}\, e^{-z/T}.$

II: $\dfrac{dN(t)}{dt} = r_0 N(t)\left[1 - \dfrac{N(t-T)}{K}\right].$

III: $N(t+T) - N(t) = r_0 T\, N(t)\left[1 - \dfrac{N(t)}{K}\right].$

IV: $N(t+T) - N(t) = r_0 T\, N(t)\left[1 - \dfrac{N(t-T)}{K}\right].$

RESULTS:	STABLE		UNSTABLE
Model	Non-oscillatory	Oscillatory	Oscillatory
I	$0 < r_0 T < \dfrac{4}{27}$	$\dfrac{4}{27} < r_0 T < 2$	$r_0 T > 2$
II	$0 < r_0 T < e^{-1}$	$e^{-1} < r_0 T < \dfrac{\pi}{2}$	$r_0 T > \dfrac{\pi}{2}$
III	$0 < r_0 T < 1$	$1 < r_0 T < 2$	$r_0 T > 2$
IV	$0 < r_0 T < \dfrac{1}{4}$	$\dfrac{1}{4} < r_0 T < 1$	$r_0 T > 1$

It is interesting how similar results turn out to be even for rather different models.

12.5 Population Growth in a Time-Varying Environment

1. Given: Random variable $Y \sim$ normal (μ, σ^2)

   Expand $\ln Y$ about $Y = \mu$ in Taylor Series

   $$\ln Y = \ln \mu + \frac{Y-\mu}{\mu} - \frac{(Y-\mu)^2}{2\mu^2} + \cdots$$

   Find expectation

   $$E(\ln Y) \doteq E\left\{\ln \mu + \frac{Y-\mu}{\mu} - \frac{(Y-\mu)^2}{2\mu^2}\right\}$$

   $$= E(\ln \mu) + \frac{1}{\mu}E(Y-\mu) - \frac{1}{2\mu^2}E(Y-\mu)^2$$

   But $E(\ln \mu) = \ln E(\mu) = \ln E(Y)$

   $$E(Y-\mu) = \mu - \mu = 0$$

   $$E\left[(Y-\mu)^2\right] = V(Y) = \sigma^2$$

   $\rightarrow$

   $$E(\ln Y) = \ln E(Y) - \frac{\sigma^2}{2\mu^2}$$

   Since $\sigma^2 > 0$, $2\mu^2 > 0 \Rightarrow E(\ln Y) < \ln E(Y)$

2. $\rho = (.9)(1.1) + (.1)(0.3) = 1.02$

   $$E(N_{100}) = \rho^{100}(N_0) = 7.24\, N_0$$

   $$\mu_{\ln Y} = (.9)\ln(1.1) + (.1)\ln(0.3) = -0.0346$$

   $$\sigma^2_{\ln Y} = (.9)\left[\ln(1.1)\right]^2 + (.1)\left[\ln(0.3)\right]^2$$
   $$- (-0.0346)^2 = 0.1519$$

   $$\sigma_{\ln Y} = \sqrt{.1519} = 0.3898$$

   Let $K_1 = N_0$, $K_2 = \infty \rightarrow$

   $$\tau_1 = \frac{\frac{1}{t}\ln \frac{N_0}{N_0} - \mu_{\ln Y}}{\sigma_{\ln Y}/\sqrt{t}} = \frac{.0346(10)}{.3898} = .8881$$

   $$\tau_2 = \infty$$

   Thus $\text{Prob}\left\{N_{100} > N_0\right\} = .187 = 18.7\%$

   $\uparrow$

   From Table of Normal Dist.

3. $\frac{dN}{dt} = r_0 N(1 - \frac{N}{K}) \rightarrow \frac{1}{N^2}\frac{dN}{dt} = \frac{r_0}{N} - \frac{r_0}{K}$.

Let $y = \frac{1}{N}$, $\frac{dy}{dt} = -\frac{1}{N^2}\frac{dN}{dt} \rightarrow \frac{dy}{dt} + r_0 y = \frac{r_0}{K}$.

Use integrating factor to solve

$$e^{r_0 t}\left\{ \frac{dy}{dt} + r_0 y \right\} = \frac{d}{dt}\left\{ y e^{r_0 t} \right\} = \frac{r_0}{K} e^{r_0 t}.$$

Integrate both sides

$$y e^{r_0 t} = \frac{r_0}{K}\int_0^t e^{r_0 \tau} d\tau + C \; : \; C = \text{Constant of Integration}$$

$$= \frac{1}{K}(e^{r_0 t} - 1) + C.$$

Initial condition $N(0) = N_0 \rightarrow y(0) = \frac{1}{N_0}$.

Thus, substituting in above equation, with $t = 0$

$$y(0) = C = \frac{1}{N_0}.$$

Hence

$$y(t) = \frac{1}{N_0} e^{-r_0 t} + \frac{1}{K}(1 - e^{-r_0 t})$$

and

$$N(t) = \left[y(t) \right]^{-1} = \frac{1}{\frac{1}{N_0} e^{-r_0 t} + \frac{1}{K}(1 - e^{-r_0 t})}$$

$$= \frac{N_0 e^{r_0 t}}{1 + \frac{N_0}{K}(e^{r_0 t} - 1)} \qquad \text{(as before)}.$$

12.6 Stable Points, Stable Cycles and Chaos

1. $N_{t+1} = N_t \left[1 + r_0 (1 - \frac{N_t}{K}) \right]$

$\equiv f\left[N_t \right] = (1 + r_0)N_t - r_0\frac{N_t^2}{K}$.

a) Fixed point: $N^{(1)} = f\left[N^{(1)} \right] \Rightarrow$

$N^{(1)} = N^{(1)} \left[1 + r_0 (1 - \frac{N^{(1)}}{K}) \right] \Rightarrow N^{(1)} = K$

(Ignore uninteresting root at $N^{(1)} = 0$).

Stability: $\lambda^{(1)} \equiv (df/dN)\big|_{N=N^{(1)}}$

$\lambda^{(1)} = (1 + r_0) - 2r_0 = 1 - r_0.$

Real for all real r_0, stable if $|\lambda^{(1)}| < 1 \leftrightarrows$

$$0 < r_0 < 2 .$$

b) $N_{t+2} = f\left[N_{t+1} \right] = f\left[f\left[N_t \right] \right] \equiv f^{(2)}\left[N_t \right]$.

$N_{t+2} = (1 + r_0)N_{t+1} - r_0 \frac{N_{t+1}^2}{K}$

$= (1 + r_0)\left[(1 + r_0)N_t - \frac{r_0}{K}N_t^2 \right]$

$\qquad - \frac{r_0}{K}\left[(1 + r_0)N_t - \frac{r_0}{K}N_t^2 \right]^2$

$= (1 + r_0)^2 N_t - \frac{r_0(1 + r_0)(2 + r_0)}{K}N_t^2$

$\qquad + \frac{2r_0^2(1 + r_0)}{K^2}N_t^3 - \frac{r_0^3}{K^3}N_t^4$.

Let $X_t \equiv \frac{N_t}{K} \rightarrow$

$X_{t+2} = (1 + r_0)^2 X_t - r_0(1 + r_0)(2 + r_0)X_t^2$

$\qquad \underbrace{+ 2r_0^2(1 + r_0)X_t^3 - r_0^3 X_t^4}$

$\qquad\qquad f^{(2)}\left[X_t \right].$

c) Fixed points: $X^{(2)} = f^{(2)}[X^{(2)}]$

$$X^{(2)} = (1 + r_0)^2 X^{(2)} - r_0(1 + r_0)(2 + r_0)(X^{(2)})^2$$
$$+ 2r_0^2(1 + r_0)(X^{(2)})^3 - r_0^3(X^{(2)})^4.$$

Clearly, two roots are $X^{(2)} = 0$ and $X^{(2)} = \dfrac{N^{(1)}}{K} = 1$.

Factor these out: first, factoring out $X^{(2)} = 0 \rightarrow$

$$r_0^3(X^{(2)})^3 - 2r_0^2(1 + r_0)(X^{(2)})^2$$
$$+ r_0(1 + r_0)(2 + r_0)X^{(2)} - (2r_0 + r_0^2).$$

Now factor out $X^{(2)} = 1$ - using synthetic division:

$$X^{(2)} - 1 \overline{\left| \begin{array}{l} r_0^3(X^{(2)})^2 - (r_0^3 + 2r_0^2)X^{(2)} + (r_0^2 + 2r_0) \\ \hline r_0^3(X^{(2)})^3 - 2r_0^2(1+r_0)(X^{(2)})^2 + r_0(1+r_0)(2+r_0)X^{(2)} - (2r_0 + r_0^2) \end{array} \right.}$$

$$\underline{r_0^3(X^{(2)})^3 - r_0^3(X^{(2)})^2}$$
$$- (r_0^3 + 2r_0^2)(X^{(2)})^2$$
$$\underline{- (r_0^3 + 2r_0^2)(X^{(2)})^2 - (r_0^3 + 2r_0^2)X^{(2)}}$$
$$(r_0^2 + 2r_0)X^{(2)}$$
$$\underline{(r_0^2 + 2r_0)X^{(2)} - (r_0^2 + 2r_0)}$$
$$0$$

Find other two roots of:

$$r_0^3(X^{(2)})^2 - (r_0^3 + 2r_0^2)X^{(2)} + (r_0^2 + 2r_0) = 0$$

$$X^{(2)}_{\frac{1}{2}} = \frac{r_0^3 + 2r_0^2 \pm \sqrt{(r_0^3 + 2r_0^2)^2 - 4r_0^3(r_0^2 + 2r_0)}}{2r_0^3}$$

$$= \frac{1}{2}\left\{ (1 + \frac{2}{r_0}) \pm \sqrt{1 - \frac{4}{r_0^2}} \right\}$$

Roots extraneous if discriminant $= 1 - \dfrac{4}{r_0^2} < 0 \Rightarrow r_0 < 2$.

Roots real if $r_0 \geq 2$, and located at:

$$N^{(2)}_{\frac{1}{2}} = \left\{ (r_0 + 2) \pm \sqrt{r_0^2 - 4} \right\} \frac{K}{2r_0}.$$

2.   Recall from above:

$$N_{t+2} = (1+r_0)^2 \, N_t - \frac{r_0(1+r_0)(2+r_0)}{K}N_t^2 + \frac{2r_0^2(1+r_0)}{K^2}N_t^3 - \frac{r_0^3}{K^3}N_t^4$$

$$\underbrace{\hspace{6cm}}$$

$$f^{(2)}[N_t].$$

Also

$$N_{\frac{1}{2}}^{(2)} = \frac{K}{2r_0} \left\{ (r_0 + 2) \pm \sqrt{r_0^2 - 4} \right\} \quad : r_0 \geq 2$$

Find $\dfrac{df^{(2)}[N]}{dN}$:

$$\frac{df^{(2)}[N]}{dN} = (1+r_0)^2 - \frac{2r_0(1+r_0)(2+r_0)}{K}N + \frac{6r_0^2(1+r_0)}{K^2}N^2$$

$$- \frac{4r_0^3}{K^3} N^3.$$

Could continue analytically by substituting expression
for $N_1^{(2)}$ or $N_2^{(2)}$ into $df^{(2)}/dN$ to get $\lambda^{(2)}[r_0]$.
Instead, evaluate $N_1^{(2)}$ with $r_0 = 2.5$ and $r_0 = 2.6$, and
then substitute into $df^{(2)}/dN$.   (N.B. could equally
well use $N_2^{(2)}$ - should get same answer.)

$$N_1^{(2)} = \frac{K}{2r_0} \left\{ (r_0+2) + \sqrt{r_0^2 - 4} \right\}$$

$\rightarrow$

$N_1^{(2)}[r_0 = 2.5] = 1.2000\, K$, $N_1^{(2)}[r_0 = 2.6] = 1.2041\, K$.

$$\lambda^{(2)}[r_0 = \bar{r}] = \frac{df^{(2)}}{dN}\bigg|_{N = N_1^{(2)}[r_0 = \bar{r}]}$$

$\rightarrow$

$\lambda^{(2)}[r_0 = 2.5] = 12.25 - 94.50 + 189.00 - 108.00 = -1.2500.$

$\lambda^{(2)}[r_0 = 2.6] = 12.9600 - 103.6875 + 207.7026$
$$- 122.7351 = -1.7600.$$

Interpolate: $\lambda^{(2)}[r_0 = r_c] = -1.5$

$$\frac{r_0 - 2.5}{2.6 - 2.5} = \frac{-1.5 - (-1.25)}{-1.76 - (-1.25)} \quad \rightarrow \quad r_c = 2.5490.$$

3a) 01423 ⇆

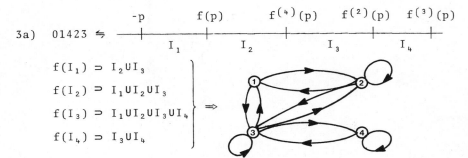

$$f(I_1) \supset I_2 \cup I_3$$
$$f(I_2) \supset I_1 \cup I_2 \cup I_3$$
$$f(I_3) \supset I_1 \cup I_2 \cup I_3 \cup I_4$$
$$f(I_4) \supset I_3 \cup I_4$$

⟹

Since graph contains period 3 digraph as a subgraph
⇒ all periods possible.

b) 01243 ⇆

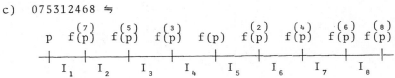

$$f(I_1) \supset I_2$$
$$f(I_2) \supset I_3 \cup I_4$$
$$f(I_3) \supset I_1 \cup I_2 \cup I_3 \cup I_4$$
$$f(I_4) \supset I_1 \cup I_2 \cup I_3$$

⟹

Since graph contains period 3 digraph as a subgraph,
⇒ all periods possible.

c) 075312468 ⇆

$$\begin{array}{ccccccccc} p & f^{(7)}(p) & f^{(5)}(p) & f^{(3)}(p) & f(p) & f^{(2)}(p) & f^{(4)}(p) & f^{(6)}(p) & f^{(8)}(p) \\ \hline I_1 & I_2 & I_3 & I_4 & I_5 & I_6 & I_7 & I_8 \end{array}$$

$$f(I_1) \supset I_5 \cup I_6 \cup I_7 \cup I_8$$
$$f(I_2) \supset I_8$$
$$f(I_3) \supset I_7$$
$$f(I_4) \supset I_6$$
$$f(I_5) \supset I_4 \cup I_5$$
$$f(I_6) \supset I_3$$
$$f(I_7) \supset I_2$$
$$f(I_8) \supset I_1$$

No cycles of period 3, 5 or 7.

12.7 Introduction to Two Species Models

1. Before DDT —

$$\left.\begin{array}{l} \dfrac{dS}{dt} = S(a-AL) \\[2mm] \dfrac{dL}{dt} = -L(b-BS) \end{array}\right\} \quad a,b,A,B > 0.$$

Equilibrium: $\dfrac{dS}{dt} = \dfrac{dL}{dt} = 0 \Rightarrow \underbrace{\left\{\begin{array}{l} S = 0 \\ L = 0 \end{array}\right\}}_{\text{trivial}}, \left\{\begin{array}{l} S = \dfrac{b}{B} \\ L = \dfrac{a}{A} \end{array}\right\}.$

After DDT —

$$\left.\begin{array}{l} \dfrac{dS^*}{dt} = S^*(a-AL^*) - kS^* \\[2mm] \dfrac{dL^*}{dt} = -L^*(b-BS^*) - kL^* \end{array}\right\} \quad a,b,A,B,k > 0.$$

Equilibrium: $\dfrac{dS^*}{dt} = \dfrac{dL^*}{dt} = 0 \Rightarrow \underbrace{\left\{\begin{array}{l} S^* = 0 \\ L^* = 0 \end{array}\right\}}_{\text{trivial}}, \left\{\begin{array}{l} S^* = \dfrac{b+k}{B} \\ L^* = \dfrac{a-k}{A} \end{array}\right\}.$

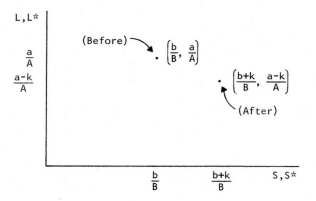

In other words, the effect of the DDT is to decrease the equilibrium level of the ladybugs (predators) and to increase the equilibrium level of the cotton cushion scale insect (prey) — the pest. This phenomenon is sometimes called Volterra's Principle.

2.
$$\frac{dR}{dt} = R(a-AR-\alpha F)$$

$$\frac{dF}{dt} = -F(b-\beta R)$$

$$\left. \right\} \quad a, A, b, \alpha, \beta > 0.$$

a. Equilibrium: $\frac{dR}{dt} = \frac{dF}{dt} = 0$

$\rightarrow R(a-AR-\alpha F) = 0$
$\qquad F(b-\beta R) = 0$
$\Rightarrow$
$\left\{\begin{matrix} R = 0 \\ F = 0 \end{matrix}\right\}, \left\{\begin{matrix} R = \frac{a}{A} \\ F = 0 \end{matrix}\right\}, \left\{\begin{matrix} R = \frac{b}{\alpha} \\ F = \frac{a}{\alpha} - \frac{Ab}{\alpha\beta} \end{matrix}\right\}.$

N.B. $(0,0) \leftrightarrows$ No animals present

$\left(\frac{a}{A}, 0\right) \leftrightarrows$ No predators, prey at carrying capacity

$\left(\frac{b}{\beta}, \frac{a}{\alpha} - \frac{Ab}{\alpha\beta}\right) \leftrightarrows$ Both species present.

b. Stability: $R^* \equiv \frac{b}{\beta}, \quad F^* \equiv \frac{a}{\alpha} - \frac{Ab}{\alpha\beta}$

Let $R(t) = R^* + r(t)$, $F(t) = F^* + f(t)$

1st Equation:

$$\frac{dr}{dt} = (R^*+r)[a - A(R^*+r) - \alpha(F^*+f)]$$

$$= \left(\frac{b}{\beta} + r\right)\left[a - A\left(\frac{b}{\beta} + r\right) - \alpha\left(\frac{a}{\alpha} - \frac{Ab}{\alpha\beta} + f\right)\right]$$

$$= \left(\frac{b}{\beta} + r\right)[-Ar - \alpha f].$$

Linearize:

$$\frac{dr}{dt} = -\frac{Ab}{\beta} r - \frac{\alpha b}{\beta} f = -AR^*r - \alpha R^*f.$$

2nd Equation:

$$\frac{df}{dt} = (F^*+f)[-b + \beta(R^*+r)]$$

$$= \left(\frac{a}{\alpha} - \frac{Ab}{\alpha\beta} + f\right)\left[-b + \beta\left(\frac{b}{\beta} + r\right)\right].$$

Linearize:

$$\frac{df}{dt} = \left(\frac{a\beta}{\alpha} - \frac{Ab}{\alpha}\right)r = \beta F^*r$$

Rewrite linearized equations in matrix form

$$\left\{\begin{matrix} \dfrac{dr}{dt} \\[2mm] \dfrac{df}{dt} \end{matrix}\right\} = \begin{bmatrix} -AR^* & -\alpha R^* \\[2mm] \beta F^* & 0 \end{bmatrix} \left\{\begin{matrix} r \\[2mm] f \end{matrix}\right\}.$$

Assume

$$\left\{\begin{matrix} r \\ f \end{matrix}\right\} = \left\{\begin{matrix} C_1 \\ C_2 \end{matrix}\right\} e^{\lambda t} \;\rightarrow\; \begin{bmatrix} -AR^* - \lambda & -\alpha R^* \\[2mm] \beta F^* & -\lambda \end{bmatrix} \left\{\begin{matrix} C_1 \\ C_2 \end{matrix}\right\} = 0$$

$$\Rightarrow \det \begin{bmatrix} -AR^* - \lambda & -\alpha R^* \\[2mm] +\beta F^* & -\lambda \end{bmatrix} = \lambda^2 + AR^*\lambda + \alpha\beta R^* F^* = 0.$$
Characteristic Equation

Thus

$$\lambda_{\frac{1}{2}} = \frac{1}{2}\{-AR^* \pm \sqrt{(AR^*)^2 - 4\alpha\beta R^* F^*}\}$$

$$= \frac{AR^*}{2}\{-1 \pm \sqrt{1-\xi^2}\} \;:\; \xi^2 = \frac{4\alpha\beta F^*}{A^2 R^*} > 0.$$

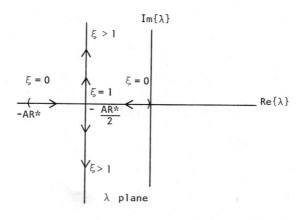

λ plane

Thus $0 < \xi < 1 \leqq$ Stable, non-oscillatory
$\xi > 1 \leqq$ Stable, oscillatory

N.B. If $A \rightarrow 0$ get back neutrally stable, oscillatory solution. $(A \rightarrow 0 \leqq K \rightarrow \infty)$.

-172-

12.8 Competition and Mutualism

1. Given

$$\frac{dX}{dt} = X(a - \alpha Y) \atop \frac{dY}{dt} = Y(b - \beta X) \Bigg\} \qquad a, b, \alpha, \beta > 0.$$

a. Equilibrium: $\dfrac{dX}{dt} = \dfrac{dY}{dt} = 0 \Rightarrow$

$$\left. \begin{aligned} X(a - \alpha Y) &= 0 \\ Y(b - \beta X) &= 0 \end{aligned} \right\} \Rightarrow \underbrace{\begin{cases} X = 0 \\ Y = 0 \end{cases}}_{\text{trivial}}, \begin{cases} X = \dfrac{b}{\beta} \\ Y = \dfrac{a}{\alpha} \end{cases}.$$

Stability: Let $X = \dfrac{b}{\beta} + x$, $Y = \dfrac{a}{\alpha} + y$

$$\to \frac{dx}{dt} = \left(\frac{b}{\beta} + x\right)\left[a - \alpha\left(\frac{a}{\alpha} + y\right)\right] = -\frac{\alpha b}{\beta} y - \alpha xy.$$

$$\frac{dy}{dt} = \left(\frac{a}{\alpha} + y\right)\left[b - \beta\left(\frac{b}{\beta} + x\right)\right] = -\frac{a\beta}{\alpha} x - \beta xy.$$

Assume $|x| \ll \dfrac{b}{\beta}$, $|y| \ll \dfrac{a}{\alpha}$ and linearize—

$$\to \begin{Bmatrix} \dfrac{dx}{dt} \\ \dfrac{dy}{dt} \end{Bmatrix} = \begin{bmatrix} 0 & -\dfrac{\alpha b}{\beta} \\ -\dfrac{a\beta}{\alpha} & 0 \end{bmatrix} \begin{Bmatrix} x \\ y \end{Bmatrix}.$$

Assume solution of form $\begin{Bmatrix} x \\ y \end{Bmatrix} = \begin{Bmatrix} A \\ B \end{Bmatrix} e^{\lambda t} \to$

$$\begin{bmatrix} -\lambda & -\dfrac{\alpha b}{\beta} \\ -\dfrac{a\beta}{\alpha} & -\lambda \end{bmatrix} \begin{Bmatrix} A \\ B \end{Bmatrix} e^{\lambda t} = 0 \Rightarrow \det \begin{bmatrix} -\lambda & -\dfrac{\alpha b}{\beta} \\ -\dfrac{a\beta}{\alpha} & -\lambda \end{bmatrix} = 0.$$

Characteristic Equation

$$\lambda^2 - ab = 0 \Rightarrow \lambda_{\frac{1}{2}} = \pm\sqrt{ab}$$

Since one root always has $\text{Re}\{\lambda\} > 0 \Rightarrow$ unstable.

b. Eliminate explicit time dependence in linearized equations

$$\frac{\frac{dy}{dt}}{\frac{dx}{dt}} = \frac{dy}{dx} = \frac{-\frac{a\beta}{\alpha}x}{-\frac{\alpha b}{\beta}y} = \left(\frac{a}{\alpha^2}\right)\left(\frac{\beta^2}{b}\right)\frac{x}{y} = \left(\frac{b}{a}\right)\left(\frac{Y^*}{X^*}\right)^2\frac{x}{y}$$

$$\text{where } \left\{X^* = \frac{b}{\beta}, \ Y^* = \frac{a}{\alpha}\right\}.$$

Separate and integrate:

$$\left(\frac{1}{Y^*}\right)^2\int y\,dy = \left(\frac{b}{a}\right)\left(\frac{1}{X^*}\right)^2\int x\,dx$$

$$\left(\frac{y}{Y^*}\right)^2 = \left(\frac{b}{a}\right)\left(\frac{x}{X^*}\right)^2 + C \ : \ C = \text{Constant of Integration.}$$

Thus

$$\left(\frac{y}{Y^*}\right)^2 - \left(\frac{b}{a}\right)\left(\frac{x}{X^*}\right)^2 = C \ : \ \text{Hyperbolas.}$$

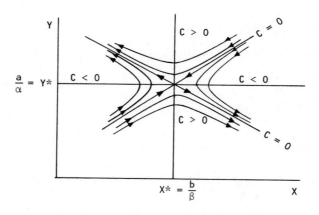

N.B. Could easily determine direction of motion along hyperbolas by looking at $\frac{dx}{dt}$ and $\frac{dy}{dt}$ at any point (x,y)—results shown on graph.

-174-

c. Isoclines and arrows—nonlinear equations

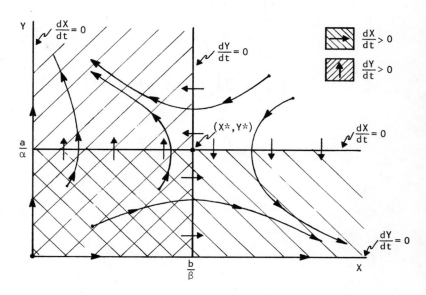

Typical solutions shown—note that there are no equilibria with just one species present.

2. Mutualism:

$$\frac{dX}{dt} = X(a - AX + \alpha Y)$$
$$\frac{dY}{dt} = Y(b - BY + \beta X)$$
$$a,b,A,B,\alpha,\beta > 0.$$

To avoid unbounded growth, require that there be an equilibrium point in 1st quadrant of X,Y space (i.e., in "population space") with both species present.

Equilibrium: $\frac{dX}{dt} = \frac{dY}{dt} = 0 \Rightarrow$

$$X(a - AX + \alpha Y) = 0$$
$$Y(b - BY + \beta X) = 0 \quad \rightarrow$$

$$AX - \alpha Y = a$$
$$- \beta X + BY = b.$$

-175-

Apply Cramer's method:

$$X = X^* = \frac{\begin{vmatrix} a & -\alpha \\ b & B \end{vmatrix}}{\begin{vmatrix} A & -\alpha \\ -\beta & B \end{vmatrix}} = \frac{aB + \alpha b}{AB - \alpha\beta}$$

$$Y = Y^* = \frac{\begin{vmatrix} A & a \\ -\beta & b \end{vmatrix}}{AB - \alpha\beta} = \frac{Ab + a\beta}{AB - \alpha\beta}$$

$$X^*, \ Y^* > 0 \iff$$

$$\underline{\underline{AB > \alpha\beta}}.$$

12.9 Quadratic Two-Species Population Models

1.   Given:

$$K(x,y) = x^\alpha y^\beta : \begin{cases} \alpha = \dfrac{b_2(b_1-a_1)}{A} - 1 \\[3mm] \beta = \dfrac{a_1(a_2-b_2)}{A} - 1. \end{cases}$$

$A \equiv a_1 b_2 - a_2 b_1.$

$B \equiv a_0 b_2(b_1-a_1) + b_0 a_1(a_2-b_2) = A\{a_0(\alpha+1) + b_0(\beta+1)\}.$

$\left. \begin{array}{l} f(x,y) = x(a_0+a_1 x+a_2 y) \\ g(x,y) = y(b_0+b_1 x+b_2 y) \end{array} \right\}$

Show that

$$\frac{\partial}{\partial x}(Kf) + \frac{\partial}{\partial y}(Kg) = \frac{B}{A} K .$$

$Kf = x^{\alpha+1} y^\beta (a_0+a_1 x+a_2 y).$

$$\frac{\partial}{\partial x}(Kf) = (\alpha+1)\underbrace{x^\alpha y^\beta (a_0+a_1 x+a_2 y)}_{\dfrac{Kf}{x}} + a_1 \underbrace{x^{\alpha+1} y^\beta}_{xK} .$$

$Kg = x^\alpha y^{\beta+1}(b_0+b_1 x+b_2 y).$

$$\frac{\partial}{\partial y}(Kg) = (\beta+1)\underbrace{x^\alpha y^\beta(b_0+b_1 x+b_2 y)}_{\dfrac{Kg}{y}} + b_2 \underbrace{x^\alpha y^{\beta+1}}_{yK} .$$

Thus

$$\frac{\partial}{\partial x}(Kf) + \frac{\partial}{\partial y}(Kg) = K\left\{ (\alpha+1)\frac{f}{x} + a_1 x + (\beta+1)\frac{g}{y} + b_2 y \right\}$$

$$= K\{ (\alpha+1)(a_0+a_1 x+a_2 y) + a_1 x$$

$$+ (\beta+1)(b_0+b_1 x+b_2 y) + b_2 y\}$$

$$= K\{a_0(\alpha+1) + b_0(\beta+1)$$

$$+ [a_1(\alpha+2) + b_1(\beta+1)]x$$

$$+ [b_2(\beta+2) + a_2(\alpha+1)]y\}.$$

Look at terms in square brackets.

$$[a_1(\alpha+2)+b_1(\beta+1)] = \frac{1}{A}\{a_1[b_2(b_1-a_1)+a_1b_2-a_2b_1]$$

$$+b_1a_1(a_2-b_2)\}$$

$$= \frac{1}{A}\{\cancel{a_1b_1b_2}-\cancel{a_1^2b_2}+\cancel{a_1^2b_2}-\cancel{a_1a_2b_1}+\cancel{a_1a_2b_1}-\cancel{a_1b_1b_2}\} = 0.$$

$$[b_2(\beta+2)+a_2(\alpha+1)] = \frac{1}{A}\{b_2[a_1(a_2-b_2)+a_1b_2-a_2b_1]$$

$$+a_2b_2(b_1-a_1)\}$$

$$= \frac{1}{A}\{\cancel{a_1a_2b_2}-\cancel{a_1b_2^2}+\cancel{a_1b_2^2}-\cancel{a_2b_1b_2}+\cancel{a_2b_1b_2}-\cancel{a_1a_2b_2}\} = 0.$$

Thus

$$\frac{\partial}{\partial x}(Kf) + \frac{\partial}{\partial y}(Kg) = K\{a_0(\alpha+1) + b_0(\beta+1)\} = \frac{B}{A}K(x,y) \quad \#$$

2. Given:

$$\left. \begin{array}{l} \dfrac{dx}{dt} = x(1 - x^2 - y^2) - y \\[2mm] \dfrac{dy}{dt} = y(1 - x^2 - y^2) + x \end{array} \right\}$$

a. Equilibrium: $\dfrac{dx}{dt} = \dfrac{dy}{dt} = 0$

$$\Rightarrow \qquad x(1-x^2-y^2) - y = 0 \Rightarrow (1-x^2-y^2) = y/x$$
$$y(1-x^2-y^2) + x = 0 \Rightarrow (1-x^2-y^2) = -x/y$$

$\Rightarrow$ only root is at $x = 0$, $y = 0$.

b. Linearized stability—linearize equations

$|x| \ll 1$, $|y| \ll 1$ $\Rightarrow$

$$\begin{array}{l} \dfrac{dx}{dt} = x - y \\[2mm] \dfrac{dy}{dt} = x + y \end{array} \quad \rightarrow \quad \begin{Bmatrix} \dot{x} \\ \dot{y} \end{Bmatrix} = \begin{bmatrix} 1 & -1 \\ 1 & 1 \end{bmatrix} \begin{Bmatrix} x \\ y \end{Bmatrix}.$$

Assume $\begin{Bmatrix} x \\ y \end{Bmatrix} = \begin{Bmatrix} A \\ B \end{Bmatrix} e^{\lambda t} \Rightarrow \begin{Bmatrix} \dot{x} \\ \dot{y} \end{Bmatrix} = \begin{Bmatrix} A \\ B \end{Bmatrix} \lambda e^{\lambda t}.$

Thus
$$\begin{bmatrix} 1-\lambda & -1 \\ 1 & 1-\lambda \end{bmatrix} \begin{Bmatrix} A \\ B \end{Bmatrix} = 0 \Rightarrow \det \begin{bmatrix} 1-\lambda & -1 \\ 1 & 1-\lambda \end{bmatrix} = 0.$$

Characteristic Equation

$(1-\lambda)^2 + 1 = 0.$

$\lambda^2 - 2\lambda + 2 = 0.$

$\lambda = \frac{1}{2}\{2 \pm \sqrt{4-8}\} = 1 \pm i \Rightarrow$ unstable and oscillatory.

c. Let $\left. \begin{array}{l} r = \sqrt{x^2+y^2} \\ \\ \theta = \tan^{-1}(y/x) \end{array} \right\} \equiv \left\{ \begin{array}{l} x = r\cos\theta \\ \\ y = r\sin\theta \end{array} \right.$

$\frac{dx}{dt} = x(1-x^2-y^2) - y.$

$\frac{dy}{dt} = y(1-x^2-y^2) + x.$

Multiply 1st equation by x, 2nd by y and add →

$x\frac{dx}{dt} + y\frac{dy}{dt} = (x^2+y^2)(1-x^2-y^2)$

but $r^2 = x^2+y^2 \rightarrow 2r\frac{dr}{dt} = 2\left[x\frac{dx}{dt} + y\frac{dy}{dt}\right].$

Thus

$r\frac{dr}{dt} = r^2(1-r^2)$ or $\frac{dr}{dt} = r(1-r^2).$

Also multiply 2nd equation by x, 1st by y and subtract

$x\frac{dy}{dt} - y\frac{dx}{dt} = x^2 + y^2$

but $\frac{y}{x} = \tan\theta \rightarrow \frac{x\frac{dy}{dt} - y\frac{dx}{dt}}{x^2} = \frac{d}{dt}\tan\theta = \frac{1}{\cos^2\theta}\frac{d\theta}{dt}$

Thus

$\frac{x^2}{\cos^2\theta}\frac{d\theta}{dt} = r^2\frac{d\theta}{dt} = r^2$ or $\frac{d\theta}{dt} = 1.$

Thus our system of equations becomes

-179-

$$\left.\begin{array}{l} \dfrac{dr}{dt} = r(1-r^2) \\[2mm] \dfrac{d\theta}{dt} = 1 \end{array}\right\}$$

<u>N.B.</u> Equations are decoupled $\Rightarrow$
Solve separately for r(t) and θ(t).

d. $\dfrac{dr}{dt} = r(1-r^2)$: Separate and integrate

$$\int_0^t dt = t = \int_{r_0}^{r(t)} \frac{dr}{r(1-r^2)}$$

Let $z = r^2$
$\quad dz = 2rdr$
$\quad \dfrac{dz}{2\sqrt{z}} = dr$.

Thus
$$t = \frac{1}{2}\int_{r_0^2}^{r^2} \frac{dz}{z(1-z)}$$

<u>N.B.</u> This is the same
integral we did for
logistic equation $\rightarrow$

$$= -\frac{1}{2}\ln\left|\frac{1-z}{z}\right|_{r_0^2}^{r^2} = -\frac{1}{2}\ln\left|\frac{(1-r^2)r_0^2}{(1-r_0^2)r^2}\right| .$$

Thus
$$\left|\frac{(1-r^2)r_0^2}{(1-r_0^2)r^2}\right| = e^{-2t} .$$

Solve for r^2

$$r^2 = \frac{1}{1 + \left[\dfrac{1-r_0^2}{r_0^2}\right]e^{-2t}} .$$

Thus
$$r(t) = \frac{r_0}{\sqrt{r_0^2 + (1-r_0^2)e^{-2t}}}$$

<u>N.B.</u> $r(t) \rightarrow 1$ as $t \rightarrow \infty$
for all r_0

$$\frac{d\theta}{dt} = 1 \rightarrow \int_{\theta_0}^{\theta(t)} d\theta = \int_0^t dt \rightarrow \theta(t) = \theta_0 + t .$$

Thus

$$(x_0, y_0) \leftrightharpoons (r_0, \theta_0)$$

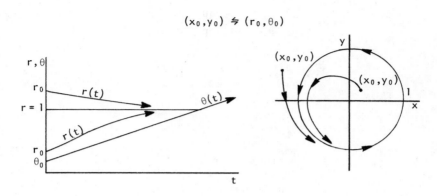

e. Equilibrium and stability analysis completely
misses the solution which is a stable limit cycle.
Note that cycle goes around an (unstable)
equilibrium point at $(0,0)$.

3. Given:

$$\frac{dx}{dt} = x \sin(x^2+y^2) - y.$$

$$\frac{dy}{dt} = y \sin(x^2+y^2) + x.$$

$$r = \sqrt{x^2+y^2} \left.\begin{matrix} \\ \\ \end{matrix}\right\} \quad \begin{cases} x = r \cos \theta \\ y = r \sin \theta \end{cases}$$

$$\theta = \tan^{-1}(y/x)$$

Transform equations $(x,y) \rightarrow (r,\theta)$

$$\frac{d}{dt}(r \cos \theta) = r \cos \theta \sin r^2 - r \sin \theta$$

$$\frac{d}{dt}(r \sin \theta) = r \sin \theta \sin r^2 + r \cos \theta$$

-181-

but

$$\frac{d}{dt}(r \cos \theta) = \cos \theta \frac{dr}{dt} - r \sin \theta \frac{d\theta}{dt}$$

$$\frac{d}{dt}(r \sin \theta) = \sin \theta \frac{dr}{dt} + r \cos \theta \frac{d\theta}{dt}.$$

Thus

$$\left[\frac{dr}{dt} - r \sin r^2\right]\cos \theta = r\left[\frac{d\theta}{dt} - 1\right]\sin \theta$$

$$\left[\frac{dr}{dt} - r \sin r^2\right]\sin \theta = -r\left[\frac{d\theta}{dt} - 1\right]\cos \theta.$$

Clearly both equations $\Rightarrow$

$$\begin{cases} \dfrac{dr}{dt} = r \sin r^2 \\[2mm] \dfrac{d\theta}{dt} = 1. \end{cases}$$

Equations are decoupled—equilibria of r occur at

$$\frac{dr}{dt} = r \sin r^2 = 0 \Rightarrow r = 0 \text{ and } \sin r^2 = 0$$

$$\Leftrightarrow r = 0, \pm\sqrt{\pi}, \pm\sqrt{2\pi}, \ldots$$

4.   Show that $H(1) = 0$.
     Consider

$$\left.\begin{array}{l} \dfrac{dx}{dt} = a_1 x + a_2 y \\[2mm] \dfrac{dy}{dt} = b_1 x + b_2 y \end{array}\right\}$$

Assume solution $x_1 = x(t)$, $y_1 = y(t)$ exists, and solution has orbit Γ_1.

But then another solution $x_2 = cx_1$, $y_2 = cy_1$ also satisfies equations:

$$\frac{dx_2}{dt} = c\frac{dx_1}{dt} = c[a_1 x_1 + a_2 y_1] = a_1 x_2 + a_2 y_2$$

$$\frac{dy_2}{dt} = c\frac{dy_1}{dt} = c[b_1 x_1 + b_2 y_2] = b_1 x_2 + b_2 y_2$$

$$\Rightarrow \quad \frac{dx_1}{dt} = a_1 x_1 + a_2 y_1 \atop \frac{dy_1}{dt} = b_1 x_1 + b_2 y_1 \Bigg\} \quad \text{which is solution} \nleftrightarrow \Gamma_1.$$

Since result is true for any constant c, if equations have periodic orbit Γ_1, also admit all orbits inside and outside $\Gamma_1 \Rightarrow$ orbit not isolated.

Next consider

$$\frac{dX}{dt} = a_0 + a_1 X + a_2 Y \atop \frac{dY}{dt} = b_0 + b_1 X + b_2 Y \Bigg\}$$

Make substitution $\begin{cases} X = x + \alpha \\ Y = y + \beta \end{cases}$: α, β to be determined

$$\rightarrow \quad \frac{dx}{dt} = a_0 + a_1(x+\alpha) + a_2(y+\beta)$$

$$\frac{dy}{dt} = b_0 + b_1(x+\alpha) + b_2(y+\beta).$$

Choose α, β such that

$$a_0 + a_1\alpha + a_2\beta = 0 \atop b_0 + b_1\alpha + b_2\beta = 0 \Bigg\} \quad \Rightarrow \quad \begin{cases} \dfrac{dx}{dt} = a_1 x + a_2 y \\[2mm] \dfrac{dy}{dt} = b_1 x + b_2 y. \end{cases}$$

Thus

$$\begin{bmatrix} a_1 & a_2 \\ b_1 & b_2 \end{bmatrix} \begin{Bmatrix} \alpha \\ \beta \end{Bmatrix} = \begin{Bmatrix} -a_0 \\ -b_0 \end{Bmatrix}.$$

Hence

$$\begin{Bmatrix} \alpha \\ \beta \end{Bmatrix} = \begin{bmatrix} a_1 & a_2 \\ b_1 & b_2 \end{bmatrix}^{-1} \begin{Bmatrix} -a_0 \\ -b_0 \end{Bmatrix} = \frac{1}{a_1 b_2 + a_2 b_1} \begin{bmatrix} b_2 & -a_2 \\ -b_1 & a_1 \end{bmatrix} \begin{Bmatrix} -a_0 \\ -b_0 \end{Bmatrix}$$

$$\alpha = \frac{a_2 b_0 - a_0 b_2}{a_1 b_2 - a_2 b_1}, \quad \beta = \frac{a_0 b_1 - a_1 b_0}{a_1 b_2 - a_2 b_1}.$$

This choice of α, β reduces equations to previous case for which there are no isolated cycles.

5.   Given

$$\frac{dx}{dt} = x - 1$$

$$\frac{dy}{dt} = 2y$$

Separate and integrate

$$\int_{x_0}^{x} \frac{dx}{x-1} = \int_0^t dt \rightarrow \quad t = \ln\left(\frac{x-1}{x_0-1}\right)$$

$$\rightarrow x(t) = 1 + (x_0-1)e^t.$$

$$\int_{y_0}^{y} \frac{dy}{y} = 2\int_0^t dt \rightarrow \quad 2t = \ln\left(\frac{y}{y_0}\right)$$

$$\rightarrow y(t) = y_0 e^{2t}.$$

Parametric solution—

$$x(t) = 1 + (x_0-1)e^t, \qquad y(t) = y_0 e^{2t}.$$

Eliminate explicit time

$$t = \ln\left(\frac{x-1}{x_0-1}\right) = \frac{1}{2}\ln\left(\frac{y}{y_0}\right) = \ln\left(\frac{y}{y_0}\right)^{\frac{1}{2}}$$

$$\rightarrow \quad \left(\frac{x-1}{x_0-1}\right) = \left(\frac{y}{y_0}\right)^{\frac{1}{2}}$$

$$y = y_0 \left(\frac{x-1}{x_0-1}\right)^2.$$

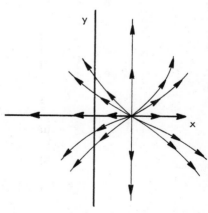

12.10 Three Species Competition

1. $\dfrac{dX}{dT} = rX(1 - \alpha_{11}X - \alpha_{12}Y)$.

$\dfrac{dY}{dT} = rY(1 - \alpha_{21}X - \alpha_{22}Y)$.

Let $x = \alpha_{11}X$, $y = \alpha_{22}Y$

$\rightarrow$

$\left.\begin{array}{l} \dfrac{dx}{dT} = rx\left[1 - x - \dfrac{\alpha_{12}}{\alpha_{22}}y\right] \\[4mm] \dfrac{dy}{dT} = ry\left[1 - \dfrac{\alpha_{21}}{\alpha_{11}}x - y\right] \end{array}\right\}$ $\begin{array}{l} a \equiv \dfrac{\alpha_{12}}{\alpha_{22}} \\[4mm] b \equiv \dfrac{\alpha_{21}}{\alpha_{11}}. \end{array}$

Also, want

$\dfrac{d(\cdot)}{dT} = \dfrac{d(\cdot)}{dt}\dfrac{dt}{dT} = r\dfrac{d(\cdot)}{dt} \Rightarrow \dfrac{dt}{dT} = r \rightarrow t = rT$.

Thus

$\left.\begin{array}{l} \dfrac{dx}{dt} = x(1 - x - ay) \\[4mm] \dfrac{dy}{dt} = y(1 - bx - y) \end{array}\right\}$ $\begin{array}{l} a \equiv \dfrac{\alpha_{12}}{\alpha_{22}} \\[4mm] b \equiv \dfrac{\alpha_{21}}{\alpha_{11}} \end{array}$ $\begin{array}{l} x = \alpha_{11}X \\ y = \alpha_{22}Y \\ t = rT. \end{array}$

2. Solve $\left.\begin{array}{l} \dfrac{dx}{dt} = x(1 - x - y) \\[4mm] \dfrac{dy}{dt} = y(1 - x - y) \end{array}\right\}$ $\begin{array}{l} x(0) = 1.5 \\[4mm] y(0) = 0.5. \end{array}$

Define $s = x + y$.

$\dfrac{dx}{dt} + \dfrac{dy}{dt} = (x+y)[1-x-y]$

$\rightarrow \qquad \dfrac{ds}{dt} = s(1-s)$.

Logistic equation $\Rightarrow s \rightarrow 1$ as $t \rightarrow \infty$.

Define $p = xy$.

$\dfrac{1}{x}\dfrac{dx}{dt} + \dfrac{1}{y}\dfrac{dy}{dt} = \dfrac{d}{dt}[\ell nxy] = 2[1-(x+y)]$

$\dfrac{d\ell np}{dt} = 2(1-s) = 2\dfrac{d\ell ns}{dt}$

-185-

$$\to \; p \; = \; p(0) \left[\frac{s}{s(0)}\right]^2 \to p(0) \left[\frac{1}{s(0)}\right]^2 \; \text{as} \; t \to \infty.$$

Next, use initial data $x(0) = 1.5, \quad y(0) = 0.5.$

$s(0) = x(0) + y(0) = 1.5 + 0.5 = 2.0.$

$p(0) = x(0) \quad y(0) = (1.5)(0.5) = 0.75.$

Thus, as $t \to \infty$

$$s \to 1 \quad \text{and} \quad p \to \frac{p(0)}{[s(0)]^2} = \frac{.75}{4} = \frac{3}{16}.$$

Hence, must solve

$$\left.\begin{array}{l} x + y = 1 \\[2mm] xy = \dfrac{3}{16} \end{array}\right\} \to x + \frac{3}{16}\frac{1}{x} = 1$$

$$\to x^2 - x + \frac{3}{16} = 0 \Rightarrow x = \frac{1}{2}\left\{1 \pm \sqrt{1 - \frac{3}{4}}\right\} = \frac{3}{4}, \frac{1}{4}.$$

Thus as $t \to \infty$

either $\qquad \left\{\begin{array}{l} x \to \dfrac{3}{4} \\[3mm] y \to \dfrac{1}{4} \end{array}\right\} \quad \text{or} \quad \left\{\begin{array}{l} x \to \dfrac{1}{4} \\[3mm] y \to \dfrac{3}{4} \end{array}\right\}.$